studysync®

Reading & Writing Companion

Turning Points

studysync®

studysync.com

Send all inquiries to:
BookheadEd Learning, LLC
610 Daniel Young Drive
Sonoma, CA 95476

Cover, ©iStock.com/brytta, ©iStock.com/Creativeye99, ©iStock.com/alexey_boldin, ©iStock.com/
skegbydave

8 9 LWI 21 20 C

STUDENT GUIDE

GETTING STARTED

Welcome to the StudySync Reading and Writing Companion! In this booklet, you will find a collection of readings based on the theme of the unit you are studying. As you work through the readings, you will be asked to answer questions and perform a variety of tasks designed to help you closely analyze and understand each text selection. Read on for an explanation of each section of this booklet.

CORE ELA TEXTS

In each Core ELA Unit you will read texts and text excerpts that share a common theme, despite their different genres, time periods, and authors. Each reading encourages a closer look with questions and a short writing assignment.

1 INTRODUCTION

An Introduction to each text provides historical context for your reading as well as information about the author. You will also learn about the genre of the excerpt and the year in which it was written.

2 FIRST READ

During your first reading of each excerpt, you should just try to get a general idea of the content and message of the reading. Don't worry if there are parts you don't understand or words that are unfamiliar to you. You'll have an opportunity later to dive deeper into the text.

3 NOTES

Many times, while working through the activities after each text, you will be asked to **annotate** or **make annotations** about what you are reading. This means that you should highlight or underline words in the text and use the "Notes" column to make comments or jot down any questions you may have. You may also want to note any unfamiliar vocabulary words here.

④ THINK QUESTIONS

These questions will ask you to start thinking critically about the text, asking specific questions about its purpose, and making connections to your prior knowledge and reading experiences. To answer these questions, you should go back to the text and draw upon specific evidence that you find there to support your responses. You will also begin to explore some of the more challenging vocabulary words used in the excerpt.

⑤ CLOSE READ & FOCUS QUESTIONS

After you have completed the First Read, you will then be asked to go back and read the excerpt more closely and critically. Before you begin your Close Read, you should read through the Focus Questions to get an idea of the concepts you will want to focus on during your second reading. You should work through the Focus Questions by making annotations, highlighting important concepts, and writing notes or questions in the "Notes" column. Depending on instructions from your teacher, you may need to respond online or use a separate piece of paper to start expanding on your thoughts and ideas.

⑥ WRITING PROMPT

Your study of each excerpt or selection will end with a writing assignment. To complete this assignment, you should use your notes, annotations, and answers to both the Think and Focus Questions. Be sure to read the prompt carefully and address each part of it in your writing assignment.

ENGLISH LANGUAGE DEVELOPMENT TEXTS

The English Language Development texts and activities take a closer look at the language choices that authors make to communicate their ideas. Individual and group activities will help develop your understanding of each text.

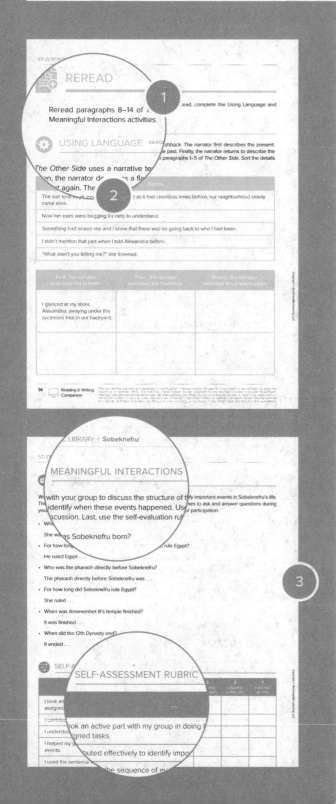

1 REREAD

After you have completed the First Read, you will have two additional opportunities to revisit portions of the excerpt more closely. The directions for each reread will specify which paragraphs or sections you should focus on.

2 USING LANGUAGE

These questions will ask you to analyze the author's use of language and conventions in the text. You may be asked to write in sentence frames, fill in a chart, or you may simply choose between multiple-choice options. To answer these questions, you should read the exercise carefully and go back in the text as necessary to accurately complete the activity.

3 MEANINGFUL INTERACTIONS & SELF-ASSESSMENT RUBRIC

After each reading, you will participate in a group activity or discussion with your peers. You may be provided speaking frames to guide your discussions or writing frames to support your group work. To complete these activities, you should revisit the excerpt for textual evidence and support. When you finish, use the Self-Assessment Rubric to evaluate how well you participated and collaborated.

EXTENDED WRITING PROJECT

The Extended Writing Project is your opportunity to explore the theme of each unit in a longer written work. You will draw information from your readings, research, and own life experiences to complete the assignment.

1 WRITING PROJECT

After you have read all of the unit text selections, you will move on to a writing project. Each project will guide you through the process of writing an argumentative, narrative, informative, or literary analysis essay. Student models and graphic organizers will provide guidance and help you organize your thoughts as you plan and write your essay. Throughout the project, you will also study and work on specific writing skills to help you develop different portions of your writing.

2 WRITING PROCESS STEPS

There are five steps in the writing process: **Prewrite**, **Plan**, **Draft**, **Revise**, and **Edit, Proofread, and Publish**. During each step, you will form and shape your writing project so that you can effectively express your ideas. Lessons focus on one step at a time, and you will have the chance to receive feedback from your peers and teacher.

3 WRITING SKILLS

Each Writing Skill lesson focuses on a specific strategy or technique that you will use during your writing project. The lessons begin by analyzing a student model or mentor text, and give you a chance to learn and practice the skill on its own. Then, you will have the opportunity to apply each new skill to improve the writing in your own project.

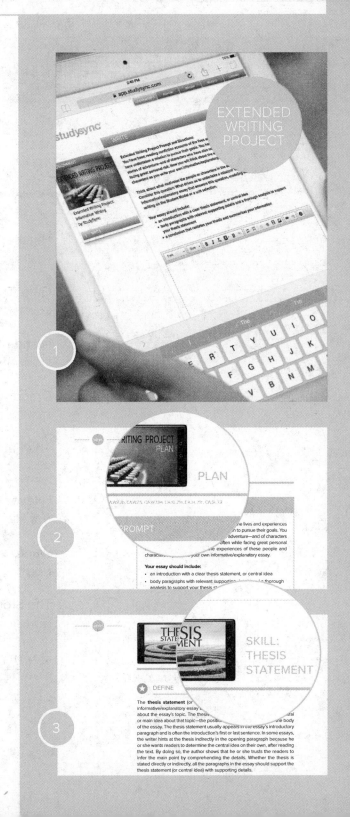

Turning Points

TEXTS

2 Reading & Writing Companion

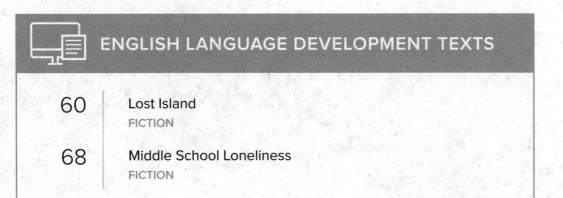

ENGLISH LANGUAGE DEVELOPMENT TEXTS

EXTENDED WRITING PROJECT

HATCHET

FICTION
Gary Paulsen
1987

INTRODUCTION

I n this gripping tale of survival by author Gary Paulsen, 13 year-old Brian is left stranded in the Canadian wilderness after his pilot has a heart attack and their plane crashes in a lake. The excerpt describes the day after the crash.

"Nothing. It kept coming back to that. He had nothing."

 FIRST READ

Excerpt from Chapter 5

1   They would look for him, look for the plane. His father and mother would be frantic. They would tear the world apart to find him. Brian had seen searches on the news, seen movies about lost planes. When a plane went down they mounted **extensive** searches and almost always they found the plane within a day or two. Pilots all filed flight plans—a detailed plan for where and when they were going to fly, with all the courses explained. They would come, they would look for him. The searchers would get government planes and cover both sides of the flight plan filed by the pilot and search until they found him.

2   Maybe even today. They might come today. This was the second day after the crash. No. Brian frowned. Was it the first day or the second day? They had gone down in the afternoon and he had spent the whole night out cold. So this was the first real day. But they could still come today. They would have started the search immediately when Brian's plane did not arrive.

3   Yeah, they would probably come today.

4   Probably come in here with **amphibious** planes, small bushplanes with floats that could land right here on the lake and pick him up and take him home.

5   Which home? The father home or the mother home. He stopped the thinking. It didn't matter. Either on to his dad or back to his mother. Either way he would probably be home by late night or early morning, home where he could sit down and eat a large, cheesy, juicy burger with tomatoes and double fries with ketchup and a thick chocolate shake.

6   And there came hunger.

7   Brian rubbed his stomach. The hunger had been there but something else—fear, pain—had held it down. Now, with the thought of the burger, the

emptiness roared at him. He could not believe the hunger, had never felt it this way. The lake water had filled his stomach but left it hungry, and now it demanded food, screamed for food.

8   And there was, he thought, absolutely nothing to eat.

9   Nothing.

10 What did they do in the movies when they got stranded like this? Oh, yes, the hero usually found some kind of plant that he knew was good to eat and that took care of it. Just ate the plant until he was full or used some kind of cute trap to catch an animal and cook it over a slick little fire and pretty soon he had a full eight-course meal.

11 The trouble, Brian thought, looking around, was that all he could see was grass and brush. There was nothing **obvious to** eat and aside from about a million birds and the beaver he hadn't seen animals to trap and cook, and even if he got one somehow he didn't have any matches so he couldn't have a fire. . .

12 Nothing.

13 It kept coming back to that. He had nothing.

14 Well, almost nothing. As a matter of fact, he thought, I don't know what I've got or haven't got. Maybe I should try and figure out just how I stand. It will give me something to do—keep me from thinking of food. Until they come to find me.

15 Brian had once had an English teacher, a guy named Perpich, who was always talking about being positive, thinking positive, staying on top of things. That's how Perpich had put it—stay positive and stay on top of things. Brian thought of him now—wondered how to stay positive and stay on top of this. All Perpich would say is that I have to get **motivated**. He was always telling kids to get motivated.

16 Brian changed position so he was sitting on his knees. He reached into his pockets and took out everything he had and laid it on the grass in front of him.

17 It was pitiful enough. A quarter, three dimes, a nickel, and two pennies. A fingernail clipper. A billfold with a twenty dollar bill—"In case you get stranded at the airport in some small town and have to buy food," his mother had said—and some odd pieces of paper.

18　And on his belt, somehow still there, the hatchet his mother had given him. He had forgotten it and now reached around and took it out and put it in the grass. There was a touch of rust already forming on the cutting edge of the blade and he rubbed it off with his thumb.

19　That was it.

20　He frowned. No, wait—if he was going to play the game, might as well play it right. Perpich would tell him to quit messing around. Get motivated. Look at *all* of it, Robeson.

21　He had on a pair of good tennis shoes, now almost dry. And socks. And jeans and underwear and a thin leather belt and a T-shirt with a windbreaker so torn it hung on him in tatters.

22　And a watch. He had a digital watch still on his wrist but it was broken from the crash—the little screen blank—and he took it off and almost threw it away but stopped the hand motion and lay the watch on the grass with the rest of it.

23　There. That was it.

24　No, wait. One other thing. Those were all the things he had, but he also had himself. Perpich used to drum that into them—"You are your most valuable **asset**. Don't forget that. *You* are the best thing you have."

25　Brian looked around again. I wish you were here, Perpich. I'm hungry and I'd trade everything I have for a hamburger.

Excerpted from Hatchet *by Gary Paulsen, published by Simon & Schuster.*

 THINK QUESTIONS　CA-CCSS: CA.RL.6.1, CA.L.6.4a, CA.L.6.4b, CA.L.6.6, CA.SL.6.1c, CA.SL.6.1d, CA.SL.6.2

1. State one or more details from the text to support your understanding of Brian's family situation— either from ideas that are directly stated or ideas that you have inferred from clues in the text.

2. How do Brian's thoughts, feelings, and reactions change as a response to what has happened to him? Cite textual evidence in your answer.

3. How does the media affect Brian's perception of what a plane crash is like? Use evidence from the text in support of your answer.

4. Use context to determine the meaning of the word **motivated** as it is used in *Hatchet*. Write your definition of "motivated" and tell how you arrived at it.

5. Remembering that the Greek prefix *amphi-* means "both" and the Greek root *bios* means "life," use the context clues provided in the passage to determine the meaning of **amphibious**. Write your definition of "amphibious" and tell how you arrived at it.

CLOSE READ

CA-CCSS: CA.RL.6.1, CA.RL.6.6, CA.W.6.5, CA.W.6.10

Reread the excerpt from *Hatchet*. As you reread, complete the Focus Questions below. Then use your answers and annotations from the questions to help you complete the Writing Prompt.

FOCUS QUESTIONS

1. Explain how the author uses the first four paragraphs to indicate Brian's realization of the severity of his situation. Highlight evidence from the text and make annotations to explain your choices.

2. Paragraph 6 consists of a single four-word sentence fragment. Why would Paulsen only include these four words in the paragraph? What do they reveal about Brian's situation? Make inferences about the text and its deeper meaning. Support your answer with textual evidence and make annotations to explain your answer choices.

3. Paragraph 10 makes a brief detour from the action as the narrator reveals Brian's thoughts about a certain kind of movie. Why is this detour a valuable addition to the narrative? Why does he think of movies at this moment? Highlight textual evidence and make annotations to explain your choices.

4. In Paragraph 14 and in the final paragraph of the excerpt, the author shows Brian's thoughts in the first person, using the pronoun *I*, as if you could read Brian's mind. What impact does this technique have in contrast to the rest of the excerpt, where Brian is called *he*? Highlight textual evidence and make annotations to explain your ideas.

5. Perpich is an important character in this excerpt despite the fact that he is not directly part of the action. Why is he important? Even though Perpich is not physically with Brian, what impact does he have on him at this life-changing moment? How does the point of view help reveal this? Highlight evidence from the text and make annotations to support your explanation.

WRITING PROMPT

How does the point of view from which Gary Paulsen tells *Hatchet* help you understand Brian's actions, thoughts, and feelings? Why do you think Paulsen chose to use Brian's third-person limited point of view rather than either Brian's first-person point of view or a third-person objective point of view? Use your understanding of point of view to think about how the story would have been different if you had read it from those other points of view. Support your writing with evidence from the text.

GUTS:
THE TRUE STORIES BEHIND HATCHET AND THE BRIAN BOOKS

NON-FICTION
Gary Paulsen
2001

INTRODUCTION

Gary Paulsen is a prolific writer of novels, short stories, plays, and magazine articles. He is best known for his series of five books about the wilderness adventures of teenager Brian Robeson, beginning with *Hatchet*. In his nonfiction work *Guts*, Paulsen shares his own real-life adventures that led to his writing *Hatchet* and other books. In this excerpt, Paulsen reflects on an experience as a volunteer emergency worker that left him with a haunting memory.

"There was, of course, hope—there is always hope."

FIRST READ

From Chapter 1: Heart Attacks, Plane Crashes and Flying

1   Perhaps the single most catastrophic event in Brian's life in *Hatchet* is when the pilot dies of a heart attack. This forces Brian to fly the plane and land—in little more than an "aimed" crash—in a lake, where he swims free and saves himself.

2   Before I was fortunate enough to become successful as a writer, I worked at home, writing as much as I could between construction jobs. Because I had so much downtime, I added my name to a list of volunteers available to answer emergency ambulance calls. My wife and I lived then in a small prairie town in the middle of farm country, near the confluence of two major highways. The volunteer service was small, and all we had was one old ambulance donated by a city that had bought new ones. But we were the only service available for thousands of square miles.

3   We answered calls to highway wrecks, farm accidents, poisonings, gunshot accidents and many, many heart attacks. I would go out on the calls alone or with another man who also worked at home.

4   I saw at least a dozen heart attack victims in the first year. Sadly, most of them were dead before I arrived. The distances we had to cover were so great that we simply could not get there in time to save them. If we did arrive before they died, we had to wait an hour or more for the "flight for life" chopper from the nearest city. Often it arrived too late.

5   When I came to write *Hatchet*, I remembered one call to a small ranch some sixty miles northeast of Colorado Springs. It was early in the morning when the siren cut loose, and I ran half-dressed for my old truck, drove to the garage where the ambulance was kept and answered the phone hanging on the wall.

Reading & Writing Companion

6   "Please come quick!" a woman said. "It's my Harvey. He's having chest pains."

7   She gave me the location of the ranch and I took off. It should have taken me a full twenty minutes to get there because of the roughness of the gravel roads but I arrived in fourteen by driving like a maniac.

8   It was just getting light as I ran into the house carrying our emergency bag, and I could smell what was happening as soon as I entered the kitchen. The lights were on and a man of about fifty was sitting at the kitchen table. His face was gray and he was holding his left shoulder with his right hand. He looked at me and smiled sheepishly, as if to apologize for the inconvenience, and started to say something but then stopped and looked again at the floor in what soldiers call the thousand-yard stare. His wife, a thin woman in jeans and a sweatshirt, stood by him, and she gave me what we called the Look—an expression that meant *Thank God you're here please save him please save him please save him.*

9   But the smell of methane was very strong and the gray look was very bad and as I reached for him to put him on his back, he jolted as if hit by electricity, stiffened in the kitchen chair and fell sideways to the floor. His eyes looked into mine. Directly into my eyes.

10   "Call the hospital and tell them to bring the chopper now," I said, and knelt to help him, but he was hit with another jolt that stiffened him and his eyes opened wide and the smell grew much stronger and I knew he was gone. There was, of course, hope—there is always hope. Even when I was called to car accidents and saw children I knew were dead, I would keep working on them because I could not bring myself to accept their death—the hope would not allow it—and I worked on this man now though the smell came up and the skin grew cold. I kept at the CPR because the woman kept giving me the Look and I could not give up hope. But minutes passed and then half an hour before I heard the sound of the rotors—which was very good time, though much too late for this man—and I kept working on him though I knew he was dead and I had seen him die, seen him move from his life into his death, and though I had seen death many times before, I had not seen it in this way. Not in the way his eyes looked into mine while the life left him.

11   Years later, when I came to write *Hatchet* and the scene where the pilot is dying, I remembered this man of all the men I saw dead from heart attacks and car wrecks and farm accidents. I remembered him and his eyes and I put him in the plane next to Brian because he was, above all things, real, and I wanted the book to be real. But I did not sleep well that night when I wrote him into the book and I will not sleep well tonight thinking of his eyes.

Excerpted from *Guts: The True Stories Behind Hatchet and the Brian Books* by Gary Paulsen, published by Laurel-Leaf Books.

THINK QUESTIONS CA-CCSS: CA.RI.6.1, CA.L.6.4a, CA.L.6.4d

1. What does the excerpt tell you about Gary Paulsen's life before he became a successful writer? Cite textual evidence in your answer.

2. From the text, what conclusions can you draw about Gary Paulsen as a person? Cite evidence from the text to support your answer.

3. What details does Gary Paulsen use to describe the appearance and expression of the wife of the heart attack victim? Why might Paulsen include these details? Cite evidence from the text to support your answer.

4. Use context clues to determine the meaning of the word **catastrophic** as it is used in *Guts: True Stories Behind* Hatchet *and the Brian Books*. Write your definition of "catastrophic" and tell how you arrived at it. Then check your meaning against the definition given in a dictionary.

5. Use context clues to determine the meaning of the word **sheepishly** as it is used in the excerpt. Write your definition of "sheepishly" and tell how you arrived at it. Then check your definition in a dictionary and revise if necessary.

CLOSE READ   CA-CCSS: CA.RI.6.1, CA.RI.6.2, CA.W.6.5, CA.W.6.10, CA.L.6.4b

Reread the excerpt from *Guts: The True Stories Behind* Hatchet *and the Brian Books*. As you reread, complete the Focus Questions below. Then use your answers and annotations from the questions to help you complete the Writing Prompt.

FOCUS QUESTIONS

1. A single paragraph may have a distinct central or main idea, separate from that of the text as a whole. What is the central idea of the first paragraph of *Guts: The True Stories Behind* Hatchet *and the Brian Books*? What details does the author include to help you determine the central idea? Highlight textual evidence to support your answer and annotate to explain your ideas.

2. In paragraph 3, Paulsen uses the word "accident" twice. The word "accident" comes from a Latin prefix, *ad-*, and a Latin root word, *cadere*. The prefix *ad-* means "toward or to," while the root *cadere* means "to fall." Given this knowledge and the context of the paragraph, what is the meaning of "accident"? Highlight clues in the text that helped you determine it.

3. In paragraph 9, how do the details the author includes support the central idea of Chapter 1? Highlight textual evidence and annotate to explain your ideas.

4. Summarize Chapter 1 of *Guts* in your own words, making sure to include the most important events or ideas without adding your personal opinions. Highlight textual evidence and annotate to explain your ideas.

5. How is the event at the ranch near Colorado Springs significant for Paulsen, and how does it become a turning point in his life? Highlight evidence from the text to support your answer and annotate to explain your ideas.

WRITING PROMPT

Reread the excerpt from *Guts: The True Stories Behind* Hatchet *and the Brian Books*, stating the central idea of the text and at least three details that support it. Note how the author uses language, particularly words with Greek and Latin roots and affixes, such as "catastrophic." How does this contribute to or support the central idea? Then, use your understanding of the central idea to describe what can happen when life changes direction. Remember to write clearly, using complete sentences and supporting your ideas with evidence from the text.

Please note that excerpts and passages in the StudySync® library and this workbook are intended as touchstones to generate interest in an author's work. The excerpts and passages do not substitute for the reading of entire texts, and StudySync® strongly recommends that students seek out and purchase the whole literary or informational work in order to experience it as the author intended. Links to online resellers are available in our digital library. In addition, complete works may be ordered through an authorized reseller by filling out and returning to StudySync® the order form enclosed in this workbook.

Reading & Writing Companion   13

ISLAND OF THE BLUE DOLPHINS

FICTION
Scott O'Dell
1960

INTRODUCTION

Based on a true story, Scott Odell's *Island of the Blue Dolphins* tells the tale of twelve-year-old Karana and her brother Ramo, who are accidentally left behind on their island home after the rest of their tribe leaves. When Ramo is killed by a pack of wild dogs, Karana must learn to survive alone. In this excerpt, Karana has just wounded the leader of the dog pack.

"I fitted an arrow and pulled back the string, aiming at his head."

 FIRST READ

Excerpt from Chapter 15

1   There were no tracks after the rain, but I followed the trail to the pile of rocks where I had seen them before. On the far side of the rocks I found the big gray dog. He had the broken arrow in his chest and he was lying with one of his legs under him.

2   He was about ten **paces** from me so I could see him clearly. I was sure that he was dead, but I lifted the spear and took good aim at him. Just as I was about to throw the spear, he raised his head a little from the earth and then let it drop.

3   This surprised me greatly and I stood there for a while not knowing what to do, whether to use the spear or my bow. I was used to animals playing dead until they suddenly turned on you or ran away.

4   The spear was the better of the two weapons at this distance, but I could not use it as well as the other, so I climbed onto the rocks where I could see him if he ran. I placed my feet carefully. I had a second arrow ready should I need it. I fitted an arrow and pulled back the string, aiming at his head.

5   Why I did not send the arrow I cannot say. I stood on the rock with the bow pulled back and my hand would not let it go. The big dog lay there and did not move and this may be the reason. If he had gotten up I would have killed him. I stood there for a long time looking down at him and then I climbed off the rocks.

6   He did not move when I went up to him, nor could I see him breathing until I was very close. The head of the arrow was in his chest and the broken **shaft** was covered with blood. The thick fur around his neck was matted from the rain.

Please note that excerpts and passages in the StudySync® library and this workbook are intended as touchstones to generate interest in an author's work. The excerpts and passages do not substitute for the reading of entire texts, and StudySync® strongly recommends that students seek out and purchase the whole literary or informational work in order to experience it as the author intended. Links to online resellers are available in our digital library. In addition, complete works may be ordered through an authorized reseller by filling out and returning to StudySync® the order form enclosed in this workbook.

Reading & Writing Companion   15

7   I do not think that he knew I was picking him up, for his body was **limp**, as if he were dead. He was very heavy and the only way I could lift him was by kneeling and putting his legs around my shoulders.

8   In this manner, stopping to rest when I was tired, I carried him to the headland.

9   I could not get through the opening under the fence, so I cut the bindings and lifted out two of the whale ribs and thus took him into the house. He did not look at me or raise his head when I laid him on the floor, but his mouth was open and he was breathing.

10 The arrow had a small point, which was **fortunate**, and came out easily though it had gone deep. He did not move while I did this, nor afterwards as I cleaned the wound with a peeled stick from a coral bush. This bush has poisonous berries, yet its wood often heals wounds that nothing else will.

11 I had not gathered food for many days and the baskets were empty, so I left water for the dog and, after mending the fence, went down to the sea. I had no thought that he would live and I did not care.

12 All day I was among the rocks gathering shellfish and only once did I think of the wounded dog, my enemy, lying there in the house, and then to wonder why I had not killed him.

13 He was still alive when I got back, though he had not moved from the place where I had left him. Again I cleaned the wound with a coral twig. I then lifted his head and put water in his mouth, which he swallowed. This was the first time that he had looked at me since the time I had found him on the trail. His eyes were sunken and they looked out at me from far back in his head.

14 Before I went to sleep I gave him more water. In the morning I left food for him when I went down to the sea, and when I came home he had eaten it. He was lying in the corner, watching me. While I made a fire and cooked my supper, he watched me. His yellow eyes followed me wherever I moved.

15 That night I slept on the rock, for I was afraid of him, and at dawn as I went out I left the hole under the fence open so he could go. But he was there when I got back, lying in the sun with his head on his paws. I had speared two fish, which I cooked for my supper. Since he was very thin, I gave him one of them, and after he had eaten it he came over and lay down by the fire, watching me with his yellow eyes that were very narrow and slanted up at the corners.

16 Four nights I slept on the rock, and every morning I left the hole under the fence open so he could leave. Each day I speared a fish for him and when I got home he was always at the fence waiting for it. He would not take the fish

from me so I had to put it on the ground. Once I held out my hand to him, but at this he backed away and showed his teeth.

17   On the fourth day when I came back from the rocks early he was not there at the fence waiting. A strange feeling came over me. Always before when I returned, I had hoped that he would be gone. But now as I crawled under the fence I did not feel the same.

18   I called out, "Dog, Dog," for I had no other name for him.

19   I ran toward the house, calling it. He was inside. He was just getting to his feet, stretching himself and yawning. He looked first at the fish I carried and then at me and moved his tail.

20   That night I stayed in the house. Before I fell asleep I thought of a name for him, for I could not call him Dog. The name I thought of was Rontu, which means in our language Fox Eyes.

Excerpted from Island of the Blue Dolphins by Scott O'Dell, published by Sandpiper.

 THINK QUESTIONS   CA-CCSS: CA.RL.6.1, CA.L.6.4a, CA.L.6.5b

1. Why does Karana, the narrator, decide not to shoot the wounded dog? Cite textual evidence to support your answer.

2. Do you think Karana has hunted with a bow and arrow before? Note evidence in the text that supports your answer.

3. Why does the dog back away and show his teeth when Karana goes up to feed him? Cite textual evidence to support your answer.

4. Use context to determine the meaning of the word **fortunate** as it is used in *Island of the Blue Dolphins*. Write your definition of "fortunate" and tell how you arrived at it. How might the word "fortunate" be related to the word "fortune"?

5. Use context clues to determine the meaning of **limp** as it is used in *Island of the Blue Dolphins*. Write your definition and note any clues that helped you to define the word. How does its relationship to other words in the sentence help you to figure out its meaning?

CLOSE READ

CA-CCSS: CA.RL.6.1, CA.RL.6.6, CA.W.6.5, CA.W.6.10

Reread the excerpt from *Island of the Blue Dolphins*. As you reread, complete the Focus Questions below. Then use your answers and annotations from the questions to help you complete the Writing Prompt.

 FOCUS QUESTIONS

1. Reread paragraphs 1 through 4. What evidence can be found in the text that suggests hunting is an important skill for Karana and others who once lived on the island? Make annotations to explain your answer.

2. Reread paragraphs 14 through 16. What evidence in the text helps to communicate the dog's feelings about Karana and the situation? Highlight evidence of the dog's actions and reactions, and make annotations to explain what they show about the dog's perspective.

3. Reread paragraphs 13 through 15. How does the author use a description of the gray dog's eyes to show the progress of his recovery in the selection? Cite textual evidence in your response.

4. Remember that Karana's brother Ramo was killed by a group of wild dogs, yet Karana seems to be uncertain about her true feelings for the gray dog she tried to kill. Highlight textual evidence that supports this statement. Why might she feel so uncertain about her true feelings?

5. What happens between Karana and the dog at the end of the selection? How do their feelings toward one another change? How might both of their lives change direction after this? Cite textual evidence to support your answer.

WRITING PROMPT

Island of the Blue Dolphins is written using first-person point of view, and everything we learn about the events in the story come from the observations of Karana, the main character. In third-person omniscient point of view, on the other hand, the narrator of the story is an observer rather than a character, and reveals the thoughts and feelings of every character in the story. How would telling Karana's encounter with the wild dog from the third person omniscient point of view reveal more information about the thoughts and feelings of both characters? Use your understanding of text evidence and point of view to arrive at your answer. Support your writing with evidence from the text.

DRAGONWINGS

FICTION
Lawrence Yep
1975

INTRODUCTION

Laurence Yep's *Dragonwings* tells the story of eight-year-old Moon Shadow, who sails from China early in the 20th century to join his father Windrider in San Francisco. Though working at a laundry, Windrider is a genius who dreams of flying. The excerpt describes the boy's yearning to be with his father.

"I knew as little about my father as I knew about the land of the Golden Mountain."

 FIRST READ

Excerpt from: The Land of the Demons
(February—March, 1903)

1   Ever since I can remember, I had wanted to know about the Land of the Golden Mountain, but my mother had never wanted to talk about it. All I knew was that a few months before I was born, my father had left our home in the Middle Kingdom, or China, as the white demons call it, and traveled over the sea to work in the demon land. There was plenty of money to be made among the demons, but it was also dangerous. My own grandfather had been **lynched** about thirty years before by a mob of white demons almost the moment he had set foot on their shores.

2   Mother usually said she was too busy to answer my questions. It was a fact that she was overworked, for Grandmother was too old to help her with the heavy work, and she had to try to do both her own work and Father's on our small farm. The rice had to be grown from seeds, and the seedlings transplanted to the paddies, and the paddies tended and harvested. Besides this, she always had to keep one eye on our very active pig to keep him from rooting in our small vegetable patch. She also had to watch our three chickens, who loved to wander away from our farm.

3   Any time I brought up the subject of the Golden Mountain, Mother suddenly found something going wrong on our farm. Maybe some seedlings had not been planted into their underwater beds properly, or perhaps our pig was eating the wrong kind of garbage, or maybe one of our chickens was dirtying our doorway. She always had some good excuse for not talking about the Golden Mountain. I knew she was afraid of the place, because every chance we got, she would take me into the small temple in our village and we would pray for Father's safety, though she would never tell me what she was afraid of. It was a small satisfaction to her that our prayers had worked so far. Mother was never stingy about burning incense for Father.

Copyright © BookheadEd Learning, LLC

4   I was curious about the Land of the Golden Mountain mainly because my father was there. I had, of course, never seen my father. And we could not go to live with him for two reasons. For one thing, the white demons would not let wives join their husbands on the Golden Mountain because they did not want us settling there permanently. And for another thing, our own **clans** discouraged wives from leaving because it would mean an end to the money the husbands sent home to their families—money which was then spent in the Middle Kingdom. The result was that the wives stayed in the villages, seeing their husbands every five years or so if they were lucky though sometimes there were longer separations, as with Mother and Father.

5   We had heavy debts to pay off, including the cost of Father's ticket. And Mother and Grandmother had decided to invest the money Father sent to us in buying more land and livestock. At any rate, there was no money to spare for Father's visit back home. But my mother never complained about the hard work or the loneliness. As she said, we were the people of the Tang, by which she meant we were a tough, hardy, patient race. (We did not call ourselves Chinese, but the people of the Tang, after that famous **dynasty** that had helped settle our area some eleven hundred years ago. It would be the same as if an English demon called himself a man of the *Tudors*, the dynasty of *Henry VIII and* of *Elizabeth I*—though demon names sound so drab compared to ours.)

6   But sometimes Mother's patience wore thin. It usually happened when we walked over to the small side room in the Temple, where classes were also held. Like many other people, Mother and Grandmother could neither read nor write; but for a small fee, the village schoolmaster would read one of Father's weekly letters to us or write a letter at our **dictation**. In the evening after dinner, we would join the line of people who had a husband or brothers or sons overseas. There we would wait until it was our turn to go inside the Temple, and Mother would nervously turn the letter over and over again in her hands until Grandmother would tell her she was going to wear out the letter before we could read it.

7   To tell the truth, I knew as little about my father as I knew about the Land of the Golden Mountain. But Mother made sure that I knew at least one important thing about him: He was a maker of the most marvelous kites. Everyone in the village said he was a master of his craft, and his kites were often treasured by their owners like family **heirlooms**. As soon as I was big enough to hold the string, Mother took me out to the hill near our village where we could fly one of Father's kites. Just the two of us would go.

8   But you won't appreciate my father's skill if you think flying a kite—any kind of a kite—is just putting a bunch of paper and sticks up into the air. I remember the first time we went to fly a kite. There was nothing like the thrill

NOTES

when my kite first leaped up out of Mother's hands into the air. Then she showed me how to pull and tug and guide the kite into the winds. And when the winds caught the kite, it shot upward. She told me then how the string in my hand was like a leash and the kite was like a hound that I had sent hunting, to flush a sunbeam or a stray **phoenix** out of the clouds.

Excerpted from *Dragonwings* by Lawrence Yep, published by HarperCollins Publishers.

THINK QUESTIONS   CA-CCSS: CA.RL.6.1, CA.L.6.4a, CA.L.6.5c

1. Refer to one or more details from the text to support your understanding of how Moon Shadow feels about the Land of the Golden Mountain—both from ideas that are directly stated and ideas that you have inferred from clues in the text.

2. Citing evidence from the text, write two or three sentences describing how Moon Shadow's mother displays strength.

3. Write two or three sentences exploring what Moon Shadow knows about his father.

4. Use context clues to determine the meaning of the word **lynched** as it is used in *Dragonwings*. Write your definition of lynched and tell how you arrived at it.

5. Use the context clues provided in the passage to determine the suggested meaning of **heirloom**. Describe the feeling that a reader might associate with "heirloom" as it is used in this context. What other words might have similar meanings and similar feelings associated with them?

CLOSE READ

CA-CCSS: CA.RL.6.1, CA.RL.6.4, CA.RL.6.6, CA.L.6.5c, CA.W.6.5, CA.W.6.10

Reread the excerpt from *Dragonwings*. As you reread, complete the Focus Questions below. Then use your answers and annotations from the questions to help you complete the Writing Prompt.

FOCUS QUESTIONS

1. As you reread the text of *Dragonwings*, remember that the story is told by eight-year-old Moon Shadow. Readers see and experience things from his point of view. In the excerpt, what details in paragraphs 1, 4, and 5 reveal Moon Shadow's point of view about the Land of the Golden Mountain and the people there? What are his ideas based on? Highlight evidence in the text, and explain how the words and phrases you've chosen reveal Moon Shadow's thoughts about the land and its people.

2. In paragraphs 2, 3, and 5, Moon Shadow describes his family's life on a small farm in China. What can you infer about their exposure to the world? How does this reality contrast with Moon Shadow's knowledge about the Land of the Golden Mountain in paragraph 1? Highlight textual evidence and make annotations to explain your choices.

3. An author may use words with particular connotations to draw an emotional response from the reader. Which words or phrases in paragraph 7 draw positive responses? How do these word choices help you understand Moon Shadow's feelings about his father? Highlight textual evidence and make annotations to explain how the word or phrase is being used.

4. In paragraph 8, which words or phrases does the author use to describe Moon Shadow's memory of flying his first kite? Highlight textual evidence and make annotations to replace words with positive connotations with words that are neutral in their associations. How would the impact of this scene on the reader be different if Yep had used more neutral words in paragraph 8?

5. Use your understanding of connotation and denotation in this excerpt to identify how the author's choice of the word "demon" has an impact on the selection, and explain what this impact is. Highlight evidence from the text and make annotations that will help support your ideas.

WRITING PROMPT

In *Dragonwings*, how do the word choices the author makes have an impact on the reader's understanding of Moon Shadow and his world? What do they reveal about Moon Shadow' point of view? Use your understanding of connotation and denotation to explain Moon Shadow's thoughts and feelings. Support your writing with evidence from the text.

THE FATHER OF CHINESE AVIATION

NON-FICTION
Rebecca Maksel
2008

INTRODUCTION

In 1903, Orville and Wilbur Wright made aviation history by becoming the first to build and fly a powered airplane. Their success fascinated Feng Ru, a Chinese immigrant and self-taught engineer living in California. Feng soon established an airplane manufacturing company in Oakland and completed his first plane in 1908. A few years later, he returned to China and continued his pioneering efforts in aviation there. Today, Feng Ru is known as the "Father of Chinese Aviation."

"Upon hearing of the Wright brothers' success, Feng turned his attention to aviation..."

FIRST READ

Feng Ru made history on the California coast, then introduced airplanes to his native land.

1   At twilight on a Tuesday evening in September 1909, Feng Ru prepared to test an airplane of his own design above the gently rolling hills of Oakland, California. It was just six years after Orville and Wilbur Wright took to the skies at Kill Devil Hills, North Carolina, and only a year after their first public flights.

2   "The big bi-plane, with its four starting wheels tucked beneath it like the talons of a bird, sailed slowly in an elliptical course around the crest of the hill nearly back to the starting point," reported the *Oakland Enquirer* in its September 23 edition. For an astonishing 20 minutes Feng circled the Piedmont area, never more than 12 feet off the ground. Suddenly, a bolt holding the propeller to the shaft snapped, sending Feng tumbling to earth, bruised but otherwise unharmed.

3   While Feng Ru is little known in the United States, his fame in China is equivalent to the Wright brothers'. Middle and high schools are named in his honor, and his childhood home is a museum; China even considers its space program to be based upon the foundations of Feng's work.

4   Feng immigrated to the U.S. from China sometime between 1894 and 1898, when he was in his early teens, and immediately set to work doing odd jobs at a Chinese mission in San Francisco. "He was staggered by America's power and prosperity. He understood that industrialization made the country great, and felt that industrialization could do the same for China," says historian Patti Gully, who has co-authored a book on the contributions of Chinese living outside their country to the development of aviation in China. "So he went east to learn all he could about machines, working in shipyards, power plants, machine shops, anywhere he could acquire mechanical knowledge."

Please note that excerpts and passages in the StudySync® library and this workbook are intended as touchstones to generate interest in an author's work. The excerpts and passages do not substitute for the reading of entire texts, and StudySync® strongly recommends that students seek out and purchase the whole literary or informational work in order to experience it as the author intended. Links to online resellers are available in our digital library. In addition, complete works may be ordered through an authorized reseller by filling out and returning to StudySync® the order form enclosed in this workbook.

Reading & Writing Companion   25

5   Feng became well known for developing alternate versions of the water pump, the generator, the telephone, and the wireless telegraph, some of which were used by San Francisco's Chinese businessmen. But upon hearing of the Wright brothers' success, Feng turned his attention to aviation, laboriously translating into Chinese anything he could find on the Wrights, Glenn Curtiss and, later, French aircraft designer Henri Farman.

6   By 1906, Feng decided to return to California to establish an aircraft factory, building airplanes of his own design. San Francisco's massive earthquake and resulting fire forced him to relocate to Oakland instead, where, funded by local Chinese businessmen, Feng erected his workshop—a 10- by eight-foot shack. Jammed into this small space were tools, books, journals, mechanical projects, aircraft parts—and Feng himself, who rarely finished work before 3 a.m.

7   In this tiny spot, the self-taught engineer established the Guangdong Air Vehicle Company in 1909, and completed his first airplane that year, according to the American Institute of Aeronautics and Astronautics. During one test flight, Feng lost control of his airplane (not an unusual occurrence), which plunged into his workshop, setting it ablaze. Feng and his three assistants moved operations to an Oakland hayfield, referred to by the *New York Times* and the *Washington Post* as "a hidden retreat."

8   "They posted guards at the perimeters of the field to discourage the curious," says Gully, "and talked to visitors through a crack in the wall."

9   So anxious was Feng to keep his invention secret that he had the engine castings made by different East Coast machine shops, then assembled the parts himself. His discretion paid off; Feng's successful test flights were covered by mainstream press, and his work was praised by revolutionary Sun Yat-sen. By 1911, as the *New York Times* reported on February 21: "[Feng] will leave here for his native land to-morrow, taking with him a biplane of the Curtiss type, in which he intends to make exhibition flights. It is believed that he will be the first aviator to rise from the ground in China. . . . The machine he is taking to China is of his own construction. The aviator is financed by six of his countrymen, residents of Oakland, who will accompany him on the trip. The first flights will be tried at Hongkong and Canton."

10   Feng was leaving just in time: anti-Chinese sentiment was on the rise in the American West, and the Oregonian reported of the pilot's latest flight: "Immigration officials and customs inspectors are today said to be gnashing their teeth. They find it hard enough to keep the Chinese out now, without having them dropping in on flying machines."

11   When Feng arrived in Hong Kong on March 21, 1911, by custom he should have headed immediately toward his ancestral village to pay his respects.

But even with his family urging him to come home, the preoccupied inventor was so obsessed with his airplane that it took him two months to fulfill his duties.

12   On August 26, 1912, Feng was killed while performing an aerial exhibition before a crowd of 1,000 spectators. "He was performing in a plane of his own design and manufacture," says Gully. "He was flying at about 120 feet and had traveled about five miles before the accident. I've read a report that he put his machine into an extreme climb, but his engine seemed to fail and the aircraft fell to the ground. It sounds like a classic stall, but of course no one knew about such things in those days. His aircraft smashed into a bamboo grove, and his injuries included a pierced lung. As he lay dying, he reportedly told his assistants, 'Your faith in the progress of your cause is by no means to be affected by my death.'"

13   The Republic of China gave Feng Ru a full military funeral, awarding him the posthumous rank of a major general. At Sun Yat-Sen's request, the words "Chinese Aviation Pioneer" were engraved upon Feng's tombstone.

First appeared on airspacemag.com on August 13, 2008.

 THINK QUESTIONS   CA-CCSS: CA.RI.6.1, CA.L.6.4a, CA.L.6.4b

1.   Cite textual evidence that Feng Ru was extremely devoted to his work of creating airplanes.

2.   State two or three details from the text to support the idea that Feng Ru was indeed "The Father of Chinese Aviation."

3.   Based on textual evidence, support the idea that being in the United States helped Feng Ru pursue his dream of designing and building an airplane.

4.   Remembering that the Latin root *avi* means "bird," use this knowledge, in addition to the context, to determine the meaning of the word **aviation** as it is used in "The Father of Chinese Aviation." Write your definition of "aviation" and tell how you got it.

5.   Remembering that the Latin suffix *-ence* means "an instance, act, or condition of," use the suffix, the root, and context clues provided in the passage to determine the meaning of **occurrence**. Write your definition of occurrence and tell how you arrived at it.

CLOSE READ CA-CCSS: CA.RI.6.1, CA.RI.6.2, CA.RI.6.4, CA.L.6.5c, CA.W.6.5, CA.W.6.10

Reread the article "The Father of Chinese Aviation." As you reread, complete the Focus Questions below. Then use your answers and annotations from the questions to help you complete the Writing Prompt.

FOCUS QUESTIONS

1. What information does paragraph 3 provide to support the idea that Feng Ru is honored in his native China? Highlight textual evidence in the paragraph and make annotations to support your answer.

2. Based on the details given in paragraphs 6 and 7, describe the difficult conditions that Feng worked in. Highlight textual evidence to support your ideas and make annotations to explain your answer choices.

3. What central idea about taking risks can be inferred from paragraphs 6 and 7 of the article? Highlight textual evidence and make annotations to explain your idea.

4. What central idea about racism can be logically inferred from paragraph 10 of the article? Highlight textual evidence and write annotations to explain your idea.

5. Paragraph 4 says that Feng Ru "was staggered by America's power and prosperity." Compare the denotation and connotation of the word *staggered*. What is the emotional impact of the word? Explain the impact that American industrialization had on Feng Ru's life. What other events influenced Feng Ru's work? Highlight textual evidence in the paragraph to support your answer.

WRITING PROMPT

The central idea of a text tells you what it is mostly about. The supporting details help you understand the central idea. Use your understanding of textual evidence to help you find the central idea that emerges in the article "The Father of Aviation." Provide two or more pieces of evidence from the text to support your idea. Is the idea explicit in the text, or did you need to infer it?

I NEVER HAD IT MADE

NON-FICTION
Jackie Robinson
1972

INTRODUCTION

In 1947, Jackie Robinson, a talented baseball player and man of great character, made history as the first African American baseball player to "break the color line" and play in modern Major League Baseball. In this excerpt from his autobiography, Robinson reflects back on his experience and its impact on American society.

"I had become the first black player in the major leagues."

FIRST READ

From the Preface: Today

1   I guess if I could choose one of the most important moments in my life, I would go back to 1947, in the Yankee Stadium in New York City. It was the opening day of the world series and I was for the first time playing in the series as a member of the Brooklyn Dodgers team. It was a history-making day. It would be the first time that a black man would be allowed to participate in a world series. I had become the first black player in the major leagues.

2   I was proud of that and yet I was uneasy. I was proud to be in the hurricane eye of a significant breakthrough and to be used to prove that a sport can't be called national if blacks are barred from it. Branch Rickey, the president of the Brooklyn Dodgers, had rudely awakened America. He was a man with high ideals, and he was also a shrewd businessman. Mr. Rickey had shocked some of his fellow baseball tycoons and angered others by deciding to smash the unwritten law that kept blacks out of the big leagues. He had chosen me as the person to lead the way.

3   It hadn't been easy. Some of my own teammates refused to accept me because I was black. I had been forced to live with snubs and rebuffs and rejections. Within the club, Mr. Rickey had put down rebellion by letting my teammates know that anyone who didn't want to accept me could leave. But the problems within the Dodgers club had been minor compared to the opposition outside. It hadn't been that easy to fight the resentment expressed by players on other teams, by the team owners, or by bigoted fans screaming "n——." The hate mail piled up. There were threats against me and my family and even out-and-out attempts at physical harm to me.

4   Some things counterbalanced this ugliness. Black people supported me with total loyalty. They supported me morally: they came to sit in a hostile audience in unprecedented numbers to make the turnstiles hum as they never had

NOTES

before at ballparks all over the nation. Money is America's God, and business people can dig black power if it coincides with green power, so these fans were important to the success of Mr. Rickey's "Noble Experiment."

5   Some of the Dodgers who swore they would never play with a black man had a change of mind, when they realized I was a good ballplayer who could be helpful in their earning a few thousand more dollars in world series money. After the initial resistance to me had been crushed, my teammates started to give me tips in how to improve my game. They hadn't changed because they liked me any better; they had changed because I could help fill their wallets.

6   My fellow Dodgers were not decent out of self-interest alone. There were heartwarming experiences with some teammates; there was Southern-born Pee Wee Reese, who turned into a staunch friend. And there were others.

7   Mr. Rickey stands out as the man who inspired me the most. He will always have my admiration and respect. Critics had said, "Don't you know that your precious Mr. Rickey didn't bring you up out of the black leagues because he loved you? Are you stupid enough not to understand that the Brooklyn club profited hugely because of what your Mr. Rickey did?"

8   Yes, I know that. But I also know what a big gamble he took. A bond developed between us that lasted long after I had left the game. In a way I feel I was the son he had lost and he was the father I had lost.

9   There was more than just making money at stake in Mr. Rickey's decision. I learned that his family was afraid that his health was being undermined by the resulting pressures and that they pleaded with him to abandon the plan. His peers and fellow baseball moguls exerted all kinds of influence to get him to change his mind. Some of the press condemned him as a fool and a demagogue. But he didn't give in.

10 In a very real sense, black people helped make the experiment succeed. Many who came to the ball park had not been baseball fans before I began to play in the big leagues. Suppressed and repressed for so many years, they needed a victorious black man as a symbol. It would help them believe in themselves. But black support of the first black man in the majors was a complicated matter. The breakthrough created as much danger as it did hope. It was one thing for me out there on the playing field to be able to keep my cool in the face of insults. But it was another for all those black people sitting in the stands to keep from overreacting when they sensed a racial slur or an unjust decision. . . . I learned from Rachel, who had spent hours in the stands, that clergymen and laymen had held meetings in the black community to spread the word. We all knew about the help of the black press. Mr. Rickey and I owed them a great deal.

NOTES

11   Children from all races came to the stands. The very young seemed to have no hangup at all about my being black. They just wanted me to be good, to deliver, to win. The inspiration of their innocence is amazing. I don't think I'll ever forget the small, shrill voice of a tiny white kid who, in the midst of a racially tense atmosphere during an early game in a Dixie town, cried out, "Attaboy, Jackie." It broke the tension and it made me feel I had to succeed.

12   The black and the young were my cheering squads. But also there were people—neither black nor young—people of all races and faiths and in all parts of the country, people who couldn't care less about my race.

13   Rachel was even more important to my success. I know that every successful man is supposed to say that without his wife he could never have accomplished success. It is gospel in my case. Rachel shared those difficult years that led to this moment and helped me through all the days thereafter. She has been strong, loving, gentle, and brave, never afraid to either criticize or comfort me.

Excerpted from *I Never Had It Made* by Jackie Robinson, published by HarperCollins Publishers.

THINK QUESTIONS   CA-CCSS: CA.RI.6.1, CA.RI.6.4, CA.L.6.4a, CA.L.6.4c

1. Refer to one or more details from the text to support your understanding of why Jackie Robinson feels uneasy about opening day of the world series—both from ideas that are directly stated and ideas that you have inferred from clues in the text.

2. Use details from the text to write two or three sentences describing the different ways people treated Jackie Robinson.

3. Write two or three sentences exploring who Jackie Robinson credits with contributing to his success and why. Support your answer with textual evidence.

4. Use context to determine the meaning of the word **shrewd** as it is used in *I Never Had It Made*. Write your definition of **shrewd** and tell how you arrived at it. Then, use a dictionary or thesaurus to find the precise definition of the word, and revise your original definition as needed.

5. Use the context clues provided in the passage to determine the meaning of the word **inspiration** as it is used in *I Never Had It Made*. Write your definition of **inspiration** and tell how you arrived at it.

CLOSE READ CA-CCSS: CA.RI.6.1, CA.RI.6.2, CA.RI.6.4, CA.RI.6.5, CA.RI.6.7, CA.L.6.5a, CA.W.6.5, CA.W.6.10

Reread the excerpt from *I Never Had It Made*. As you reread, complete the Focus Questions below. Then use your answers and annotations from the questions to help you complete the Writing Prompt.

 FOCUS QUESTIONS

Question 3 asks you to use documents located on the web. Ask your teacher for URLs to find these documents. You can find it on YouTube or through another source.

1. In paragraph 3, Robinson describes his treatment by teammates and players on other teams. What can you infer about their view of African Americans in baseball? How does this treatment contrast with the responses of children in paragraph 11? How does this information contribute to your understanding of what Robinson experienced? Highlight evidence in the text to support your ideas and write annotations to explain your choices.

2. An author may use figurative language to express strong emotions or to add interest to the text. Which words or phrases in the text show the range of emotions Robinson experienced? Highlight your evidence and annotate to explain how each word or phrase is important.

3. View the video clip "Rachel Robinson: Meeting Branch Rickey". Which parts of the text does the video elaborate on? What new information about the relationship between Robinson and Branch Rickey did you learn from the video? Highlight your evidence and annotate to show what more you understand about Robinson and Branch Rickey after viewing the video.

4. In paragraph 11, use your understanding of text structure to explain the cause and effect relationship Robinson presents and how it contributes to the development of ideas. Highlight evidence in the text to support your ideas and write annotations to explain your choices.

5. Remember that the story is told by Jackie Robinson. Readers see and experience things through this one individual. In the text, what details in paragraphs 2, 4, and 10 reveal why Robinson's selection as the first black player in the major leagues was significant and contribute to the development of the ideas in the text? What impact did his selection have on the American culture? What did this change mean for different groups of people? Highlight evidence in the text and make annotations to explain why Robinson's selection is historically important.

WRITING PROMPT

Compare and contrast the video clip about Jackie Robinson's role in the Civil Rights Movement and the excerpt from *I Never Had It Made*. How are the two alike, and how do they differ? Be sure to comment on how each medium is structured and the kinds of language each one features. Does figurative language play a role in both? If not, does any element of the video fill the same role as the figures of speech in the text? How do the video and text support the overall message of what constitutes a turning point in life? Support your writing with evidence from the text and video.

WARRIORS DON'T CRY

NON-FICTION
Melba Pattillo Beals
1994

INTRODUCTION

In 1954, the Supreme Court decision *Brown* v. *the Board of Education of Topeka, Kansas* declared that segregation was unconstitutional and schools must be integrated. To thwart the efforts of the Arkansas governor to keep the first nine black students, including Melba Pattillo Beals, out of Central High School, President Eisenhower sent federal troops to Little Rock to make sure the students got in safely. In this excerpt, Beals describes how the soldiers escorted them through the crowds into the school.

"The soldiers did not make eye contact as they surrounded us..."

 FIRST READ

1   The next morning, Wednesday, September 25, at 8 A.M., as we turned the corner near the Bateses' home, I saw them, about fifty uniformed soldiers of the 101st. Some stood still with their rifles at their sides, while others manned the jeeps parked at the curb. Still other troops walked about holding walkie-talkies to their ears. As I drew nearer to them I was fascinated by their well-shined boots. Grandma had always said that well-kept shoes were the mark of a disciplined individual. Their guns were also glistening as though they had been polished, and the creases were sharp in the pant legs of their uniforms.

2   I had heard all those newsmen say "Screaming Eagle Division of the 101st", but those were just words. I was seeing human beings, flesh-and-blood men with eyes that looked back at me. They resembled the men I'd seen in army pictures on TV and on the movie screen. Their faces were white, their expressions blank.

3   There were lots of people of both races standing around, talking to one another in whispers. I recognized some of the ministers from our churches. Several of them nodded or smiled at me. I was a little concerned because many people, even those who knew me well, were staring as though I were different from them.

4   Thelma and Minnijean stood together inspecting the soldiers close up while the other students milled about. I wondered what we were waiting for. I was told there was an assembly at Central with the military briefing the students.

5   Reporters hung from trees, perched on fences, stood on cars and darted about with their usual urgency. Cameras were flashing on all sides. There was an **eerie** hush over the crowd, not unlike the way I'd seen folks behave outside the home of the deceased just before a funeral.

6 There were tears in Mother's eyes as she whispered good-bye. "Make this day the best you can," she said.

7 "Let's bow our heads for a word of prayer." One began to say some comforting words. I noticed tears were streaming down the faces of many of the adults. I wondered why they were crying and just at that moment when I had more hope of staying alive and keeping safe than I had since the **integration** began.

8 "Protect those youngsters and bring them home. Flood the Holy Spirit into the hearts and minds of those who would attack our children."

9 "Yes, Lord," several voices echoed.

10 One of the soldiers stepped forward and beckoned the driver of a station wagon to move it closer to the driveway. Two jeeps moved forward, one in front of the station wagon, one behind. Guns were mounted on the hoods of the jeeps.

11 We were already a half hour late for school when we heard the order "Move out" and the leader motioned us to get into the station wagon. As we collected ourselves and walked toward the caravan, many of the adults were crying openly. When I turned to wave to Mother Lois, I saw tears streaming down her cheeks. I couldn't go back to comfort her.

12 Sarge, our driver, was friendly and pleasant. He had a Southern accent, different from ours, different even from the one Arkansas whites had. We rolled away from the curb lined with people waving at us. Mama looked even more **distraught**. I remembered I hadn't kissed her good-bye.

13 Our convoy moved through streets lined with people on both sides, who stood as though they were waiting for a parade. A few friendly folks from our community waved as we passed by. Some of the white people looked totally horrified, while others raised their fists to us. Others shouted ugly words.

14 We pulled up to the front of the school. Groups of soldiers on guard were lined at intervals several feet apart. A group of twenty or more was running at breakneck speed up and down the street in front of Central High School, their rifles with bayonets pointed straight ahead. Sarge said they were doing crowd control—keeping the mob away from us.

15 About twenty soldiers moved toward us, forming an olive-drab square with one end open. I glanced at the faces of my friends. Like me, they appeared to be impressed by the **imposing** sight of military power. There was so much to see, and everything was happening so quickly. We walked through the open end of the square. Erect, rifles at their sides, their faces stern, the soldiers did not

NOTES

make eye contact as they surrounded us in a protective cocoon. After a long moment, the leader motioned us to move forward.

16   I felt proud and sad at the same time. Proud that I lived in a country that would go this far to bring justice to a Little Rock girl like me, but sad that they had to go to such great lengths. Yes, this is the United States, I thought to myself. There is a reason that I salute the flag. If these guys just go with us this first time, everything's going to be okay.

17   We began moving forward. The eerie silence of that moment would be forever etched into my memory. All I could hear was my own heartbeat and the sound of boots clicking on the stone.

18   Everyone seemed to be moving in slow motion as I peered past the raised **bayonets** of the 101st soldiers. I walked on the concrete path toward the front door of the school, the same path the Arkansas National Guard had blocked us from days before. We approached the stairs, our feet moving in unison to the rhythm of the marching click-clack sound of the Screaming Eagles. Step by step we climbed upward-where none of my people had ever before walked as a student. We stepped up the front door of Central High School and crossed the threshold into that place where angry segregationist mobs had forbidden us to go.

Excerpted from *Warriors Don't Cry* by Melba Pattillo Beals, published by Washington Square Press.

THINK QUESTIONS   CA-CCSS: CA.RI.6.1, CA.L.6.4a, CA.L.6.4c

1.   Refer to one or more details from the text to support your understanding of why soldiers are escorting Beals and other students—both from ideas that are directly stated and ideas that you have inferred from clues in the text.

2.   Write two or three sentences exploring how the presence of the students affected different individuals in the crowd in different ways. Cite evidence from the text in your sentences.

3.   Cite evidence from the text that shows how Beals feels about being escorted through the crowds.

4.   Use context clues to determine the meaning of the word **distraught** as it is used in *Warriors Don't Cry*. Write your definition of *distraught* and tell how you arrived at it. Then, use a dictionary to confirm the precise pronunciation of "distraught." Why might this word be challenging to pronounce if a reader is not familiar with it?

5.   Using context clues provided in the passage, define **bayonets** and explain how you got your definition. Then, use a dictionary to determine the precise meaning and pronunciation of the word. Are the precise meaning and pronunciation what you expected? Explain.

CLOSE READ CA-CCSS: CA.RI.6.1, CA.RI.6.2, CA.RI.6.5, CA.W.6.5, CA.W.6.10

Reread the excerpt from *Warriors Don't Cry*. As you reread, complete the Focus Questions below. Then use your answers and annotations from the questions to help you complete the Writing Prompt.

FOCUS QUESTIONS

1. Reread paragraph 2 of the text. How does Beals portray the difference between hearing about a historical event on the news and actually living through it? Highlight words and phrases that show the contrast, and write annotations that explain these differences. How does paragraph 5 build on this contrast?

2. In paragraph 12 of the text, Beals makes a point to mention that she hadn't kissed her mother good-bye. Why was it important for her to share this with readers? What can you infer from this detail? Why is this information significant? Cite evidence from the text to support your answer.

3. Throughout the text, Beals never lets readers forget that soldiers are guarding her and her fellow classmates. Cite evidence from the text to explain what these soldiers represent. How do these details contribute to the central idea of the text?

4. Explain why the last two paragraphs of the selection are significant to the time order structure that Beals has laid out in the text. How might their impact change if Beals had begun her story with these paragraphs and then described what happened before them? Highlight parts of the text that support your answer.

5. Why was the experience of crossing the threshold into Central High School a life-changing event for Beals and other African Americans? What impact did her experiences on that day have on her feelings about her country? Highlight textual evidence to support your answer.

WRITING PROMPT

Identify the central idea of the excerpt and describe how the author's use of a sequential text structure helps her develop that central idea effectively. Then choose two to three paragraphs from the text and explain the essential role that each one plays in the text structure. What does each paragraph contribute to the sequence of events that Beals describes? How do your selected paragraphs add memorable facts and details to her account of this turning point in her life? What conclusion can you draw about her experience? Be sure to support your ideas with textual evidence.

THE STORY OF MY LIFE

NON-FICTION
Helen Keller
1903

INTRODUCTION

Serious illness at the age of 19 months left Helen Keller both blind and deaf. Serving as an inspiration to millions, Keller overcame those handicaps and went on to become a renowned author and social activist. In this passage from her autobiography, six-year-old Helen meets the person who will change her life forever, her private teacher Anne Sullivan.

"'Light! give me light!' was the wordless cry of my soul."

FIRST READ

Excerpt from Chapter IV

1   The most important day I remember in all my life is the one on which my teacher, Anne Mansfield Sullivan, came to me. I am filled with wonder when I consider the immeasurable contrasts between the two lives which it connects. It was the third of March, 1887, three months before I was seven years old.

2   On the afternoon of that eventful day, I stood on the porch, dumb, expectant. I guessed vaguely from my mother's signs and from the hurrying to and fro in the house that something unusual was about to happen, so I went to the door and waited on the steps. The afternoon sun penetrated the mass of honeysuckle that covered the porch, and fell on my upturned face. My fingers lingered almost unconsciously on the familiar leaves and blossoms which had just come forth to greet the sweet southern spring. I did not know what the future held of marvel or surprise for me. Anger and bitterness had preyed upon me continually for weeks and a deep languor had succeeded this passionate struggle.

3   Have you ever been at sea in a dense fog, when it seemed as if a tangible white darkness shut you in, and the great ship, tense and anxious, **groped** her way toward the shore with plummet and sounding-line, and you waited with beating heart for something to happen? I was like that ship before my education began, only I was without compass or sounding-line, and had no way of knowing how near the harbour was. "Light! give me light!" was the wordless cry of my soul, and the light of love shone on me in that very hour.

4   I felt approaching footsteps. I stretched out my hand as I supposed to my mother. Some one took it, and I was caught up and held close in the arms of her who had come to **reveal** all things to me, and, more than all things else, to love me.

5   The morning after my teacher came she led me into her room and gave me a doll. The little blind children at the Perkins **Institution** had sent it and Laura Bridgman had dressed it; but I did not know this until afterward. When I had played with it a little while, Miss Sullivan slowly spelled into my hand the word "d-o-l-l." I was at once interested in this finger play and tried to imitate it. When I finally succeeded in making the letters correctly I was flushed with childish pleasure and pride. Running downstairs to my mother I held up my hand and made the letters for doll. I did not know that I was spelling a word or even that words existed; I was simply making my fingers go in monkey-like imitation. In the days that followed I learned to spell in this uncomprehending way a great many words, among them pin, hat, cup and a few verbs like sit, stand and walk. But my teacher had been with me several weeks before I understood that everything has a name.

6   One day, while I was playing with my new doll, Miss Sullivan put my big rag doll into my lap also, spelled "d-o-l-l" and tried to make me understand that "d-o-l-l" applied to both. Earlier in the day we had had a tussle over the words "m-u-g" and "w-a-t-e-r." Miss Sullivan had tried to impress it upon me that "m-u-g" is mug and that "w-a-t-e-r" is water, but I persisted in **confounding** the two. In despair she had dropped the subject for the time, only to renew it at the first opportunity. I became impatient at her repeated attempts and, seizing the new doll, I dashed it upon the floor. I was keenly delighted when I felt the fragments of the broken doll at my feet. Neither sorrow nor regret followed my passionate outburst. I had not loved the doll. In the still, dark world in which I lived there was no strong **sentiment** or tenderness. I felt my teacher sweep the fragments to one side of the hearth, and I had a sense of satisfaction that the cause of my discomfort was removed. She brought me my hat, and I knew I was going out into the warm sunshine. This thought, if a wordless sensation may be called a thought, made me hop and skip with pleasure.

7   We walked down the path to the well-house, attracted by the fragrance of the honeysuckle with which it was covered. Some one was drawing water and my teacher placed my hand under the spout. As the cool stream gushed over one hand she spelled into the other the word water, first slowly, then rapidly. I stood still, my whole attention fixed upon the motions of her fingers. Suddenly I felt a misty consciousness as of something forgotten--a thrill of returning thought; and somehow the mystery of language was revealed to me. I knew then that "w-a-t-e-r" meant the wonderful cool something that was flowing over my hand. That living word awakened my soul, gave it light, hope, joy, set it free! There were barriers still, it is true, but barriers that could in time be swept away.

8   I left the well-house eager to learn. Everything had a name, and each name gave birth to a new thought. As we returned to the house every object which I touched seemed to quiver with life. That was because I saw everything with

NOTES

the strange, new sight that had come to me. On entering the door I remembered the doll I had broken. I felt my way to the hearth and picked up the pieces. I tried vainly to put them together. Then my eyes filled with tears; for I realized what I had done, and for the first time I felt repentance and sorrow.

9   I learned a great many new words that day. I do not remember what they all were; but I do know that mother, father, sister, teacher were among them-- words that were to make the world blossom for me, "like Aaron's rod, with flowers." It would have been difficult to find a happier child than I was as I lay in my crib at the close of that eventful day and lived over the joys it had brought me, and for the first time longed for a new day to come.

THINK QUESTIONS   CA-CCSS: CA.RI.6.1, CA.L.6.4a, CA.L.6.4b, CA.SL.6.1a, CA.SL.6.1c

1. How did Helen Keller's disabilities affect her before her teacher, Anne Sullivan, arrived? Support your answer with evidence from the text.

2. Did Anne Sullivan give Helen the doll simply as a present, or as a way to start her education? Refer to text evidence to support your answer.

3. Why is the episode at the well such a significant moment in Keller's life? Support your answer with details from the text.

4. Use context clues to determine the meaning of the word **reveal** as it is used in *The Story of My Life*. Write your definition of reveal and tell how you arrived at it.

5. The Latin root *in-* + *statuere* means "to set up." Use this information and context in the passage to determine the meaning of **institution**. Write your definition of institution and tell how you arrived at it.

CLOSE READ   CA-CCSS: CA.RI.6.1, CA.RI.6.2, CA.RI.6.4, CA.RI.6.5, CA.L.6.5c, CA.W.6.5, CA.W.6.10

Reread the excerpt from *The Story of My Life*. As you reread, complete the Focus Questions below. Then use your answers and annotations from the questions to help you complete the Writing Prompt.

FOCUS QUESTIONS

1. Writers of informational text often use the exact, or denotative, meaning of a word to construct literal meaning. In an autobiography, writers sometimes use the connotative meaning of a word when they tell about emotional moments in their own lives. In the sixth paragraph of *The Story of My Life*, Helen Keller recalls the "passionate outburst" she had when she took a doll Anne Sullivan had given her and dashed it to the floor. Keller also uses the word *passionate* in the second paragraph. Does this use of the word have a positive or negative connotation? Use textual evidence to support your answer.

2. In paragraph 2, Keller uses the word "languor" to describe the way she felt just before Anne Sullivan arrived. Use context clues in the sentence to define the word **languor**. Then use this text evidence to decide if the word has a more positive or more negative connotation as it is used here. Use a dictionary or thesaurus to confirm your definition. What word or words might have a similar meaning, but a different connotation?

3. The word *flushed* is a word that can have multiple denotative meanings: to drive from cover or from a hiding place; to turn red or blush; to clean or empty; a sudden feeling of emotion, such as excitement, pride, or anger. What meaning of the word *flushed* does Helen Keller use in the fifth paragraph? Does it have a positive or a negative connotation? Use evidence from the text to support your answer.

4. Most authors of informational text use a specific text structure to organize and present information. What text structure does Keller use throughout this excerpt? Cite textual evidence and annotate to support your answer.

5. In paragraph 7, Sullivan holds one of Keller's hands under a running waterspout and traces letters spelling "water" on Keller's other hand. How did this moment change Keller? How does this event support the central idea that Anne Sullivan opened up the world to Helen Keller? Highlight textual evidence and annotate to support your answer.

WRITING PROMPT

Keller experiences a change of emotions between paragraphs 6 and 8. How does the author's use of connotation in the text help the reader understand her change in feelings? How does her change relate to the central idea in the text? Support your writing with evidence from the text. Be sure to include words with positive and negative connotations from the paragraphs as textual evidence.

ELEVEN

FICTION
Sandra Cisneros
1991

INTRODUCTION

When her teacher insists that an ugly red sweater belongs to Rachel, the eleven year-old has exceptional thoughts, but can't share them. Even so, it's evident that the protagonist of Sandra Cisnero's short story has insight beyond her years.

"I'm eleven and it's my birthday today and I'm crying like I'm three…"

 FIRST READ

1   What they don't understand about birthdays and what they never tell you is that when you're eleven, you're also ten, and nine, and eight, and seven, and six, and five, and four, and three, and two, and one. And when you wake up on your eleventh birthday you expect to feel eleven, but you don't. You open your eyes and everything's just like yesterday, only it's today. And you don't feel eleven at all. You feel like you're still ten. And you are—underneath the year that makes you eleven.

2   Like some days you might say something stupid, and that's the part of you that's still ten. Or maybe some days you might need to sit on your mama's lap because you're scared, and that's the part of you that's five. And maybe one day when you're all grown up maybe you will need to cry like if you're three, and that's okay. That's what I tell Mama when she's sad and needs to cry. Maybe she's feeling three.

3   Because the way you grow old is kind of like an onion or like the rings inside a tree trunk or like my little wooden dolls that fit one inside the other, each year inside the next one. That's how being eleven years old is.

4   You don't feel eleven. Not right away. It takes a few days, weeks even, sometimes even months before you say Eleven when they ask you. And you don't feel smart eleven, not until you're almost twelve. That's the way it is.

5   Only today I wish I didn't have only eleven years rattling inside me like pennies in a tin Band-Aid box. Today I wish I was one hundred and two instead of eleven because if I was one hundred and two I'd have known what to say when Mrs. Price put the red sweater on my desk. I would've known how to tell her it wasn't mine instead of just sitting there with that look on my face and nothing coming out of my mouth.

6 "Whose is this?" Mrs. Price says, and she holds the red sweater up in the air for all the class to see. "Whose? It's been sitting in the coatroom for a month."

7 "Not mine," says everybody. "Not me."

8 "It has to belong to somebody," Mrs. Price keeps saying, but nobody can remember. It's an ugly sweater with red plastic buttons and a collar and sleeves all stretched out like you could use it for a jump rope. It's maybe a thousand years old and even if it belonged to me I wouldn't say so.

9 Maybe because I'm skinny, maybe because she doesn't like me, that stupid Sylvia Saldivar says, "I think it belongs to Rachel." An ugly sweater like that, all raggedy and old, but Mrs. Price believes her. Mrs. Price takes the sweater and puts it right on my desk, but when I open my mouth nothing comes out.

10 "That's not, I don't, you're not . . . Not mine," I finally say in a little voice that was maybe me when I was four.

11 "Of course it's yours," Mrs. Price says, "I remember you wearing it once." Because she's older and the teacher, she's right and I'm not.

12 Not mine, not mine, not mine, but Mrs. Price is already turning to page thirty-two, and math problem number four. I don't know why but all of a sudden I'm feeling sick inside, like the part of me that's three wants to come out of my eyes, only I squeeze them shut tight and bite down on my teeth real hard and try to remember today I am eleven, eleven. Mama is making a cake for me for tonight, and when Papa comes home everybody will sing Happy birthday, happy birthday to you.

13 But when the sick feeling goes away and I open my eyes, the red sweater's still sitting there like a big red mountain. I move the red sweater to the corner of my desk with my ruler. I move my pencil and books and eraser as far from it as possible. I even move my chair a little to the right. Not mine, not mine, not mine.

14 In my head I'm thinking how long till lunchtime, how long till I can take the red sweater and throw it over the schoolyard fence, or leave it hanging on a parking meter, or bunch it up into a little ball and toss it in the alley. Except when math period ends Mrs. Price says loud and in front of everybody, "Now, Rachel, that's enough," because she sees I've shoved the red sweater to the tippy-tip corner of my desk and it's hanging all over the edge like a waterfall, but I don't care.

15   "Rachel," Mrs. Price says. She says it like she's getting mad. "You put that sweater on right now and no more nonsense."

16   "But it's not—"

17   "Now!" Mrs. Price says.

18   This is when I wish I wasn't eleven, because all the years inside of me—ten, nine, eight, seven, six, five, four, three, two, and one—are pushing at the back of my eyes when I put one arm through one sleeve of the sweater that smells like cottage cheese, and then the other arm through the other and stand there with my arms apart like if the sweater hurts me and it does, all itchy and full of germs that aren't mine.

19   That's when everything I've been holding in since this morning, since when Mrs. Price put the sweater on my desk, finally lets go, and all of a sudden I'm crying in front of everybody. I wish I was invisible but I'm not. I'm eleven and it's my birthday today and I'm crying like I'm three in front of everybody. I put my head down on the desk and bury my face in my stupid clown-sweater arms. My face all hot and spit coming out of my mouth because I can't stop the little animal noises from coming out of me, until there aren't any more tears left in my eyes, and it's just my body shaking like when you have the hiccups, and my whole head hurts like when you drink milk too fast.

20   But the worst part is right before the bell rings for lunch. That stupid Phyllis Lopez, who is even dumber than Sylvia Saldivar, says she remembers the red sweater is hers! I take it off right away and give it to her, only Mrs. Price pretends like everything's okay.

21   Today I'm eleven. There's a cake Mama's making for tonight, and when Papa comes home from work we'll eat it. There'll be candles and presents and everybody will sing Happy birthday, happy birthday to you, Rachel, only it's too late.

22   I'm eleven today. I'm eleven, ten, nine, eight, seven, six, five, four, three, two, and one, but I wish I was one hundred and two. I wish I was anything but eleven, because I want today to be far away already, far away like a runaway balloon, like a tiny o in the sky, so tiny-tiny you have to close your eyes to see it.

THINK QUESTIONS   CA-CCSS: CA.RL.6.1, CA.L.6.4a, CA.L.6.4b

1. How does Rachel feel about the red sweater that is placed on her desk? Respond with textual evidence from the story as well as ideas that you have inferred from clues in the text.

2. According to Rachel, why does Sylvia say the sweater belongs to Rachel? Support your answer with textual evidence.

3. Write two or three sentences exploring why Mrs. Price responds as she does when Phyllis claims the sweater. Support your answer with textual evidence.

4. Use context clues to determine the meaning of the word **raggedy** as it is used in *Eleven*. Write your definition of "raggedy" and tell how you arrived at it.

5. Remembering that the Latin prefix *non-* means "not, or the reverse of," use the context clues provided in the passage to determine the meaning of **nonsense**. Write your definition of "nonsense" and tell how you arrived at it.

CLOSE READ

CA-CCSS: CA.RL.6.1, CA.RL.6.4, CA.RL.6.5, CA.RL.6.6, CA.L.6.5a, CA.W.6.5, CA.W.6.10

Reread the short story "Eleven." As you reread, complete the Focus Questions below. Then use your answers and annotations from the questions to help you complete the Writing Prompt.

FOCUS QUESTIONS

1. As you reread the text of "Eleven," remember that the story is told by the main character, eleven-year-old Rachel. In the first four paragraphs of the story, Rachel uses the second-person point of view by referring to readers as "you." Why do you think the author of the story chose to structure the story that way? Highlight details in the text and make annotations that support your thinking.

2. Beginning in paragraph 5, Rachel begins to tell readers the story from a first person point of view. Why does she do this? How does the change affect the structure of the story? Highlight evidence from the text and make annotations that support your thinking.

3. Reread paragraph 12. What figure of speech does the author use in this paragraph? What does this figure of speech mean? Make annotations to explain how you interpret this figure of speech, and highlight evidence from the text that supports your interpretation.

4. The author uses a figure of speech called a *simile* to compare two things that seem dissimilar, but that share certain qualities. Reread paragraph 19 and explain why "my whole head hurts like when you drink milk too fast" is an effective simile. Annotate your ideas using evidence from the text.

5. In the last paragraph, Rachel repeats an idea that she told readers at the beginning of the story. What idea does she repeat? How does this add to your understanding of Rachel and her experience? Why has this experience been a turning point for her? Highlight textual evidence and make annotations to explain your choices.

WRITING PROMPT

In "Eleven," Sandra Cisneros focuses the narrative on an embarrassing moment in the life of the main character. Analyze how that choice contributes to the overall development of the plot. What do we learn about Rachel through her description of this event that we might not otherwise know? How does the way Cisneros structures the story help build sympathy for Rachel? How do figures of speech such as similes contribute to the descriptions of Rachel and reveal her ideas about her world? How does the event support Rachel's theory that people are all the ages they've ever been? Support your writing with evidence from the text. Be sure to cite specific examples of similes and other figures of speech that contribute to your ideas.

Please note that excerpts and passages in the StudySync® library and this workbook are intended as touchstones to generate interest in an author's work. The excerpts and passages do not substitute for the reading of entire texts, and StudySync® strongly recommends that students seek out and purchase the whole literary or informational work in order to experience it as the author intended. Links to online resellers are available in our digital library. In addition, complete works may be ordered through an authorized reseller by filling out and returning to StudySync® the order form enclosed in this workbook.

THE PIGMAN

FICTION

Paul Zindel
1968

INTRODUCTION

While making prank calls soliciting donations to an imaginary charity, high school friends John and Lorraine dial the number of Mr. Angelo Pignati. The Pigman, as they come to know him, eagerly prolongs the conversation and agrees to donate money, inviting the youths to come by his house and pick up a check. In doing so, John and Lorraine discover a lonely, eccentric man with whom they might just develop a friendship.

"There were blue, black, yellow, orange, striped, green, and rainbow-colored pigs."

 FIRST READ

 NOTES

From Chapter 5

1 "We should all go to the zoo tomorrow," Mr. Pignati said, again out of nowhere.

2 "Mr. Pignati," I said with an air of impatience, "Miss Truman and I have many other stops to make today. I mean, where would the L & J Fund be if we simply sat around . . . all day and went to zoos?"

3 "Yes," Lorraine said. "We really shouldn't have stayed this long."

4 "Oh, I'm sorry," Mr. Pignati said, and I couldn't help feeling sorry. His smile and bright eyes faded in front of us, and he got awkwardly to his feet. "Let me get the check," he said, and his voice was so depressed I thought he was really going to cry.

5 "You don't really have to—" Lorraine started, but he looked bewildered.

6 "Of course, that's what we came for," I said to make it look real at least. Lorraine shot me a look of outrage.

7 "Of course," he said.

8 We watched him go down another hall to a room that had black curtains on the doorway. I mean, there was no door, just these curtains. He disappeared through them. When he finally came back out, he seemed to be very tired, and he started writing the check.

9 "Whom should I make it out to?" he asked.

10 Lorraine gulped and went speechless.

11 "Cash will be fine. Make it out to cash," I found myself saying.

Please note that excerpts and passages in the StudySync® library and this workbook are intended as touchstones to generate interest in an author's work. The excerpts and passages do not substitute for the reading of entire texts, and StudySync® strongly recommends that students seek out and purchase the whole literary or informational work in order to experience it as the author intended. Links to online resellers are available in our digital library. In addition, complete works may be ordered through an authorized reseller by filling out and returning to StudySync® the order form enclosed in this workbook.

Reading & Writing Companion   **51**

12   He handed me the check, and my hand shook a little. It wasn't that I was scared or anything, but it was an awful lot of money.

13   "On behalf of the L & J Fund I accept this check."

14   "Oh, *yes*," Lorraine echoed, and I could tell she was furious with me because her eyes were starting to flit all over the place again.

15   "Do you think you might like to go to the zoo with me *someday*?" Mr. Pignati asked just as I knew Lorraine was getting ready to flee out of the house.

16   "I always go to the zoo." The old man laughed. "I love animals. My wife and I both love animals, but . . . I've been going to the zoo by myself lately. I always go. Every day."

17   "You love animals . . . ?" Lorraine muttered, her left hand opening the front door just a crack.

18   There was a dreadful pause.

19   "Oh, I forgot to show you my pigs!" he exclaimed, the gleam returning to his eyes. "You didn't see my pigs, did you?"

20   There came another terrible pause.

21   "No . . . we didn't see . . . your pigs," I said.

22   He gestured us back into the living room and then moved down the hall to the room at the far end—the one with the black curtains hanging on the side of the entrance. Lorraine didn't want to follow him, but I dragged her behind me until we got to the doorway.

23   "Ohh-h-h!" Lorraine stammered.

24   The room was dark because its two windows were covered with faded paper shades. It was a real dump except for the table and chairs at the far end of it. The table had pigs all over it. And the shelves had pigs all over them. There were pigs all over the place. It was ridiculous. I never saw so many pigs. I don't mean the live kind; these were phony pigs. There were glass pigs and clay pigs and marble pigs.

25   Lorraine reached her hand out.

26   "Touch them," he told her. "Don't be afraid to pick them up." It was a big change from my mother who always lets out a screech if you go near anything, so I couldn't help liking this old guy even if he was sort of weird.

27 There were pigs that had *Made in Japan* on them. Some were from Germany and Austria and Switzerland. There were pigs from Russia and lots of pigs from Italy, naturally. There were little pigs and big pigs. Ugly ones and cute ones. There were blue, black, yellow, orange, striped, green, and rainbow-colored pigs. Pigs, pigs, pigs!

28 "Don't you like them?" he asked.

29 "Oh, everybody loves pigs," I said.

30 "My wife collects pigs. I got her started on it when I gave her one to remind her of me—before we got married."

31 "Oh?"

32 "This one," he said, lifting a large white pig with an ugly smile on its face, "this one was the first one I got her. She thought it was very funny. Pig. *Pig*nati. Do you get it?"

33 "Yes, Mr. Pignati. We get it."

From Chapter Six

34 John had called the Pigman and made arrangements for us to meet him in front of the zoo at ten o'clock in the morning. We didn't want to be seen walking around our neighborhood with him, but the zoo was far enough away so we knew we'd be safe once we got there.

35 John and I arrived around nine thirty and sat down on the benches at the entrance. The sea-lion pool is right there, and that kept John busy while I was combing my hair and polishing my Ben Franklin sunglasses. I don't wear all crazy clothes, but I do like my Ben Franklin sunglasses because everyone looks at me when I wear them. I used to be afraid to have people look at me, but ever since I met John I seem to wear little things that make them look. He wears phony noses and moustaches and things like that. He's even got a big pin that says "MY, YOU'RE UGLY," and he wears that once in awhile.

36 I really didn't want to go to the zoo. I don't like seeing all those animals and birds and fish behind bars and glass just so a lot of people can stare at them. And I particularly hate the Baron Park Zoo because the attendants there are not intelligent. They really aren't. The thing that made me stop going to the zoo a few years ago was the way one attendant fed the sea lions. He climbed up on the big diving platform in the middle of the pool and unimaginatively just dropped the fish into the water. I mean, if you're going to feed sea lions, you're not supposed to plop the food into the tank. You can tell by the

Please note that excerpts and passages in the StudySync® library and this workbook are intended as touchstones to generate interest in an author's work. The excerpts and passages do not substitute for the reading of entire texts, and StudySync® strongly recommends that students seek out and purchase the whole literary or informational work in order to experience it as the author intended. Links to online resellers are available in our digital library. In addition, complete works may be ordered through an authorized reseller by filling out and returning to StudySync® the order form enclosed in this workbook.

Reading & Writing Companion   **53**

expressions on their faces that the sea lions are saying things like "Don't dump the fish in!"

37 "Pick the fish up one by one and throw them into the air so we can chase after them."

38 "Throw the fish in different parts of the tank!"

39 "Let's have fun!"

40 "Make a game out of it!"

41 If my mother had ever let me have a dog, I think it would have been the happiest dog on earth. I know just how the minds of animals work—just the kind of games they like to play. The closest I ever came to having a pet was an old mongrel that used to hang around the neighborhood. I thought there was nothing wrong with sitting on the front steps and petting him, but my mother called the ASPCA, and I know they killed him.

42 At ten o'clock sharp, Mr. Pignati arrived.

43 "Hi!" he said. His smile stretched clear across his face. "Hope I'm not late?"

44 "Right on time, Mr. Pignati. Right on time," John answered.

Excerpted from *The Pigman* by Paul Zindel, published by HarperCollins Publishers.

 THINK QUESTIONS CA-CCSS: CA.RL.6.1, CA.L.6.4a, CA.L.6.4b

1. How would you describe the narrators of *The Pigman*? Cite textual evidence to support your answer.

2. How does John react to the pigs when he first sees them in Mr. Pignati's room? Cite a sentence from the text to support your answer.

3. How does Lorraine feel about accepting Mr. Pignati's check? Cite a sentence from the text to support your answer.

4. Use context to determine the meaning of the word **behalf** as it is used in *The Pigman*. Write your definition of "behalf" and tell how you arrived at it.

5. Remembering that the Latin prefix *un-* means "not," the Latin suffix *-ive* means "of, relating to," and the Latin suffix *-ly* indicates an adverb, use the context clues provided in the passage to determine the meaning of **unimaginatively**. Write your definition of "unimaginatively" and tell how you arrived at it.

CLOSE READ   CA-CCSS: CA.RL.6.1, CA.RL.6.4, CA.RL.6.6, CA.L.6.5c, CA.W.6.5, CA.W.6.10

Reread the excerpt from *The Pigman*. As you reread, complete the Focus Questions below. Then use your answers and annotations from the questions to help you complete the Writing Prompt.

FOCUS QUESTIONS

1. What is John's view of Mr. Pignati? Does it change over the course of the text? Highlight evidence in the text and make annotations to support your answer.

2. In Chapter 5, why does John accept Mr. Pignati's check? Highlight textual evidence that supports your ideas, and write annotations to explain your answer choices.

3. In paragraph 14, John says that Lorraine was "furious" with him. What do the connotations of the word *furious* tell you about Lorraine's feelings that a synonym such as *angry* or *upset* wouldn't tell you? Highlight evidence in the text and make annotations to support your answer.

4. In paragraph 35, Lorraine presents her view of John. How has John changed Lorraine's way of behaving? Highlight evidence that shows Lorraine's point of view on the subject. Write annotations to explain your choices.

5. Write two or three sentences describing what you learn from the text about Mr. Pignati's character traits. How was meeting John and Lorraine a life-changing event for Mr. Pignati? Highlight textual evidence that supports your answer, and annotate to explain your ideas.

WRITING PROMPT

How do the two points of view from which *The Pigman* is narrated help you to better understand the characters in the story? How is this more effective than if the story were told from only one point of view? Give specific examples, and support your writing with evidence from the text.

Please note that excerpts and passages in the StudySync® library and this workbook are intended as touchstones to generate interest in an author's work. The excerpts and passages do not substitute for the reading of entire texts, and StudySync® strongly recommends that students seek out and purchase the whole literary or informational work in order to experience it as the author intended. Links to online resellers are available in our digital library. In addition, complete works may be ordered through an authorized reseller by filling out and returning to StudySync® the order form enclosed in this workbook.

Reading & Writing Companion   **55**

THE ROAD NOT TAKEN

POETRY
Robert Frost
1915

INTRODUCTION

Robert Frost's classic poem is generally interpreted as a nod to non-conformism, but some see it differently. When asked about the *sigh* in the last stanza, Frost wrote to a friend, "It was my rather private jest at the expense of those who might think I would yet live to be sorry for the way I had taken in life."

"I took the one less traveled by…"

 FIRST READ

 NOTES

1 Two roads **diverged in** a yellow wood,
2 And sorry I could not travel both
3 And be one traveler, long I stood
4 And looked down one as far as I could
5 To where it bent in the **undergrowth;**

6 Then took the other, as just as fair,
7 And having perhaps the better **claim,**
8 Because it was grassy and wanted wear;
9 Though as for that the passing there
10 Had worn them really about the same,

11 And both that morning equally lay
12 In leaves no step had **trodden** black.
13 Oh, I kept the first for another day!
14 Yet knowing how way leads on to way,
15 I doubted if I should ever come back.

16 I shall be telling this with a sigh
17 Somewhere ages and ages **hence:**
18 Two roads diverged in a wood, and I—
19 I took the one less traveled by,
20 And that has made all the difference.

THINK QUESTIONS   CA-CCSS: CA.RL.6.1, CA.L.6.4a

1. What evidence in the text of the poem shows you that the speaker is uncertain about which road to choose?

2. What do lines 16–20 tell you about how the speaker imagines his future? Explain using evidence from the text to support your answer.

3. How does the speaker feel about the road he didn't take? Cite textual evidence to support your answer.

4. Use context clues to determine the meaning of the word **trodden** as it is used in "The Road Not Taken." Write your definition of "trodden" and state the clue(s) from the text you used to determine your answer.

5. The word **diverged** is used in lines 1 and 18. What meaning of "diverged" would you guess from line 1, and how would its use in lines 18–19 help you confirm the meaning?

CLOSE READ
CA-CCSS: CA.RL.6.1, CA.RL.6.4, CA.RL.6.5, CA.RL.6.7, CA.W.6.2a, CA.W.6.2b, CA.W.6.5, CA.W.6.10

Reread the poem "The Road Not Taken." As you reread, complete the Focus Questions below. Then use your answers and annotations from the questions to help you complete the Writing Prompt.

FOCUS QUESTIONS

1. How does the poetic structure Frost uses help to unify the poem? Highlight textual evidence and make annotations to explain your ideas.

2. Highlight examples of imagery in stanza 1. What effect does this create for the reader? Cite specific textual evidence and make annotations to support your response.

3. In stanza 4, how is the poet's use of repetition effective? Highlight evidence from the text and write annotations to support your ideas.

4. What can you infer about the speaker's thoughts and feelings in this poem? Highlight evidence from the text and write annotations to support your findings.

5. The "road" in Frost's poem serves as a symbol of the journey of life. What message does Frost want the reader to understand about this journey? How is this a turning point? What can you infer about the speaker's thoughts and feelings about life's journey in this poem? Highlight evidence from the text and write annotations to support your findings.

WRITING PROMPT

How does Robert Frost's use of poetic structure and poetic elements in "The Road Not Taken" support the poem's meaning in both the print and audio versions of the poem? Explain what you believe the poem means, and how the poem's meaning is shaped by at least one aspect of poetic structure and at least one poetic element. Examine whether or not you experience these differently when you listen to the audio version, and whether hearing the poem read aloud changes your understanding of its meaning. Introduce your response with a thesis statement, and support your ideas with clearly organized details and quotations from the text.

Copyright © BookheadEd Learning, LLC

LOST ISLAND

English Language
Development

FICTION

INTRODUCTION

Mariana wakes up alone, thirsty, and hungry on a deserted island. How did she get here, and why is her head throbbing? As she slowly recalls a large wave smashing into Uncle Merlin's fishing boat, Mariana takes her first steps toward survival.

"She was trapped. Stuck. Alone. Was she going to die on this horrible island?"

FIRST READ

1   Mariana woke up slowly.

2   She was on her back. She felt sand in her mouth, in between her teeth. The air was hot and **damp**. Where am I? Her head was throbbing. Was that the smell of salt in the air, and did I just hear a seagull cry?

3   Turning her head to one side, Mariana opened her eyes. The bright light was too **intense** for her. At first, all she saw was damp yellow sand—sand and a big broken seashell that had sharp edges. She scanned her surroundings. Stones, weeds, and a few palm trees decorated the landscape. She could see the entire island. It was no larger than a soccer field.

4   Then Mariana remembered. She remembered fishing for flounder with Uncle Merlin. They found a good spot, so they **anchored** their boat near a little island. The summer morning was warm, and the bay was calm. Mariana and Merlin got their fishing lines ready, when suddenly an enormous, thundering wave came out of nowhere. The wave overturned the boat, tossing Mariana and her uncle into the water. She remembered rising to the surface and seeing land. She swam toward it; she swam and swam. An eternity seemed to have passed. She remembered thinking: Why don't I just give up? What had motivated her to keep swimming? She had finally reached the shore and had crawled up onto the sand. Exhausted.

5   Presently, Mariana looked at her surroundings, while she tried to clear her mind of the swirling thoughts. She must have passed out and slept on the beach for hours. The boat had **capsized** in early morning, but now the sun was high in the sky. It must be about noon.

6   Noon, and hot.

7   Mariana wondered where her uncle was. Why hasn't he come to get me? What is he waiting for? She felt her empty stomach; her mouth was dry. She

thought of the lunch her uncle had packed. A cool drink and an overstuffed sandwich would be perfect right now!

8   Then her reality became clear. Maybe her uncle wasn't coming to get her because maybe he had drowned. Maybe no **rescuer** was coming to get her. She was trapped. Stuck. Alone. Was she going to die on this horrible island?

9   Mariana started to cry, but she stopped herself quickly. Wait. She **cautioned** herself. Don't act like a baby. Use your head. That's what Uncle Merlin always said: "Use your head!"

10 Slowly Mariana turned onto her stomach and used her elbows to lift herself. Next, she got onto her knees and gradually stood up onto both feet. The throbbing in her head continued, but she looked into the island and took a step.

USING LANGUAGE   CA-CCSS: ELD.PII.6.5.Ex

Complete the chart by writing the correct answers in the second and third columns.

Statement with Some Detail Options	Statement with More Detail Options
She stopped suddenly.	She stopped suddenly, seeing the danger.
She slept uncomfortably.	She slept uncomfortably, disturbed by uneasy dreams.
She shook her head anxiously.	She shook her head anxiously, repeatedly.

Basic Statement	Statement with Some Detail	Statement with More Detail
She shook her head.		
She slept.		
She stopped.		

MEANINGFUL INTERACTIONS CA-CCSS: ELD.PII.6.1.Ex

Work with your partner or group to identify time clues in the following paragraphs of "Lost Island" and complete the sentences. Use the self-assessment rubric to evaluate your participation in the activity.

3 Turning her head to one side, Mariana opened her eyes. The _____ was too intense for her. _____, all she saw was damp yellow sand—sand and a big broken seashell that had sharp edges. She scanned her surroundings. Stones, weeds, and a few palm trees decorated the landscape. She could see the entire island. It was no larger than a soccer field.

4 _____ Mariana _____. She remembered fishing for flounder with Uncle Merlin. They found a good spot, so they anchored their boat near a little island. The _____ _____was warm, and the bay was calm. Mariana and Merlin got their fishing lines ready, when _____ an enormous, thundering wave came out of nowhere. The wave overturned the boat, tossing Mariana and her uncle into the water. She remembered rising to the surface and seeing land. She swam toward it; she swam and swam. An _____. She remembered thinking: Why don't I just give up? What had motivated her to keep swimming? She _____ the shore and had crawled up onto the sand. Exhausted.

5 _____, Mariana looked at her surroundings, while she tried to clear her mind of the swirling thoughts. She must have _____and _____ on the beach _____. The boat had capsized in _____, but now the sun was _____. It must be _____.

6 _____, and _____.

 SELF-ASSESSMENT RUBRIC CA-CCSS: ELD.PII.6.1.Ex

	4 I did this well.	3 I did this pretty well.	2 I did this a little bit.	1 I did not do this.
I took an active part with others in doing the assigned task.				
I contributed effectively to the group's decisions.				
I understood the use of time clue words in the selection.				
I helped others understand the use of time clue words in the selection.				
I completed the time clues sentences carefully and accurately.				

Please note that excerpts and passages in the StudySync® library and this workbook are intended as touchstones to generate interest in an author's work. The excerpts and passages do not substitute for the reading of entire texts, and StudySync® strongly recommends that students seek out and purchase the whole literary or informational work in order to experience it as the author intended. Links to online resellers are available in our digital library. In addition, complete works may be ordered through an authorized reseller by filling out and returning to StudySync® the order form enclosed in this workbook.

Reading & Writing Companion 63

REREAD

Reread paragraphs 1–5 of "Lost Island." After you reread, complete the Using Language and Meaningful Interactions activities.

USING LANGUAGE

The chart below shows different thoughts and feelings that Mariana had. Complete the chart by writing the quotations from "Lost Island" in the correct column to show how the words in the passage expressed her emotions. One has been done for you.

Quotations	
Maybe her uncle wasn't coming to get her because maybe he had drowned.	She was trapped. Stuck. Alone.
She swam toward it; she swam and swam.	Why hasn't he come to get me?
Was that the smell of salt in the air?	Was she going to die on this horrible island?
Wait. She cautioned herself. Don't be a baby. Use your head.	The throbbing in her head continued, but she looked into the island and took a step.

Confusion	Fear	Determination
Where am I?		

Reading & Writing Companion

MEANINGFUL INTERACTIONS   CA-CCSS: ELD.PI.6.1.Ex, ELD.PI.6.6.a.Ex, ELD.PII.6.1.Ex

The story "Lost Island" is told in both present time and in flashback. What part of the story is told in flashback? How would the story be different if it had been told all in present time? Discuss these answers with your partner, using the speaking frames. Then, use the self-assessment rubric to evaluate your participation in the discussion.

- One place the story is a flashback is . . .

- Another flashback is . . .

- If there had been no flashbacks, the story could have started with this event: . . .

- Because of the flashback, the reader feels . . . because Mariana felt . . .

- If the story had no flashbacks, it would be different because . . .

SELF-ASSESSMENT RUBRIC   CA-CCSS: ELD.PI.6.4.Ex

	4 I did this well.	3 I did this pretty well.	2 I did this a little bit.	1 I did not do this.
I expressed my ideas about the flashback clearly.				
I listened carefully to my partner's ideas about the flashback.				
I spoke respectfully when disagreeing with my partner.				
I was courteous when persuading my partner to share my view.				

Please note that excerpts and passages in the StudySync® library and this workbook are intended as touchstones to generate interest in an author's work. The excerpts and passages do not substitute for the reading of entire texts, and StudySync® strongly recommends that students seek out and purchase the whole literary or informational work in order to experience it as the author intended. Links to online resellers are available in our digital library. In addition, complete works may be ordered through an authorized reseller by filling out and returning to StudySync® the order form enclosed in this workbook.

Reading & Writing Companion   **65**

REREAD

Reread paragraphs 6–10 of "Lost Island." After you reread, complete the Using Language and Meaningful Interactions activities.

USING LANGUAGE

Using the Joining Word, combine the two sentences to form a single complete sentence.

Two Sentences	Joining Word	Complete Sentence
She felt her empty stomach. Her mouth was dry.	and	
The boat had capsized in early morning. Now the sun was high in the sky.	but	
A cool drink would be perfect right now! A sandwich would be perfect right now!	and	
She was trapped. Stuck.	and	
Mariana started to cry. She stopped herself quickly.	but	

MEANINGFUL INTERACTIONS CA-CCSS: ELD.PI.6.6.a.Ex, ELD.PI.6.9.Ex, ELD.PII.6.1.Ex

The author uses flashback in "Lost Island." How does flashback help the reader understand the story? How does switching between present time and flashback create different moods in the story? Work with your partners to practice sharing and discussing your answers, using the speaking frames.

- The flashback helps the reader understand the story because . . .

- Switching between present time and a flashback creates different moods such as . . . in the flashback and . . . in present time.

- An example of the . . . mood is . . .

MIDDLE SCHOOL LONELINESS

English Language Development

FICTION

INTRODUCTION

When his father accepts a new job in a different city, a boy is forced to start life over at a new school. His classmates and basketball teammates are slow to accept this outsider. Then he has a chance to help two star players. What will he choose to do?

"The team members were old, close friends. I was new there and from a different background."

FIRST READ

1   I used to think I had it made. I was captain of a winning basketball team and president of the math club.

2   Then one summer, my dad accepted a job in a different city, and we relocated. Worry rained down and soaked into my life, as I left behind my best friends. Like me, they spoke Spanish at home, ate the same foods, and loved basketball. I worried because I would be among strangers who might not understand my background. My first day in the new school proved my fears were **accurate.**

3   Aside from the school building being so large, I was the only Hispanic student. I asked students for help, but their looks said I wasn't welcome. The first week was terrible because I was completely **isolated.** No one spoke to me, and no one sat with me at lunch.

4   Then I saw a notice from Coach Wilson about basketball tryouts. Instantly, I felt at home on the court as I raced up and down trying to impress Coach. He wanted me on the team but warned me things might not be easy. The team members were old, close friends. I was new there and from a different background. Though I felt proud to be on a team again, Coach's words left me deeply uneasy.

5   The first practice was disappointing, like other experiences at that school. Jeremy was team captain, and his best friend Nathan was a good player. Jeremy shouted orders to everyone except me. Finally Coach blew the whistle and called for a team meeting. He described new plays and said that Jeremy was expected to pass the ball to me. I was supposed to make some baskets. I knew Jeremy and Nathan didn't think I could be a valuable team member, but Coach had spoken and his word was law on the court.

6   Although we played together, I had no friends on the team. One day I overheard Jeremy and Nathan struggling with an assignment in math class. I heard them say if they didn't pass Friday's test, they'd get kicked off the team. I thought seriously about their problem. We couldn't afford to lose great players. Sure they treated me badly, but they were in trouble. Besides, I wanted to win the championship game. I offered to help them with their homework; they accepted.

7   We began working together on the court and off. The team started winning every game, and **enthusiastic** students came to cheer us on. Jeremy's and Nathan's math grades went up like skyrockets. I didn't sit alone at lunch anymore because my teammates sat with me. Going to a new school is not easy, but I coped with the challenges and I **succeeded**.

USING LANGUAGE CA-CCSS: ELD.PII.6.3.Ex

Complete the chart by writing the correct answers in the second, third and fourth columns. The first row has been done for you.

Present Progressive Form Options	Past Progressive Form Options	Future Progressive Form Options
We are walking. I am laughing. He is cooking. She is playing.	I was laughing. We were walking. She was playing. He was cooking.	She will be playing. He will be cooking. We will be walking. I will be laughing.

Past Tense Verb	Present Progressive Form	Past Progressive Form	Future Progressive Form
watched	They are watching.	They were watching.	They will be watching.
played			
laughed			
walked			
cooked			

Please note that excerpts and passages in the StudySync® library and this workbook are intended as touchstones to generate interest in an author's work. The excerpts and passages do not substitute for the reading of entire texts, and StudySync® strongly recommends that students seek out and purchase the whole literary or informational work in order to experience it as the author intended. Links to online resellers are available in our digital library. In addition, complete works may be ordered through an authorized reseller by filling out and returning to StudySync® the order form enclosed in this workbook.

Reading & Writing Companion   71

MEANINGFUL INTERACTIONS   CA-CCSS: ELD.PI.6.6.a.Ex

Work with your partner to identify the turning point in "Middle School Loneliness." Choose the paragraph number that represents the turning point. Then write the sentences that represent the turning point. Use the self-assessment rubric to evaluate your participation in the activity.

5   Jeremy was team captain, and his best friend Nathan was a good player. Jeremy shouted orders to everyone except me. Finally Coach blew the whistle and called for a team meeting. He described new plays and said that Jeremy was expected to pass the ball to me.

6   One day I overheard Jeremy and Nathan struggling with an assignment in math class. I heard them say if they didn't pass Friday's test, they'd get kicked off the team. I thought seriously about their problem. We couldn't afford to lose great players. Sure they treated me badly, but they were in trouble. Besides, I wanted to win the championship game. I offered to help them with their homework; they accepted.

7   We began working together on the court and off. The team started winning every game, and enthusiastic students came to cheer us on. Jeremy's and Nathan's math grades went up like skyrockets. I didn't sit alone at lunch anymore because my teammates sat with me.

Paragraph _____   Turning Point _____

_____

_____

SELF-ASSESSMENT RUBRIC   CA-CCSS: ELD.PI.8.4.Ex

	4 I did this well.	3 I did this pretty well.	2 I did this a little bit.	1 I did not do this.
I took an active part with my partner in doing the assigned task.				
I contributed effectively to our decisions.				
I understood the turning point in the selection.				
I helped my partner understand the turning point words in the selection. (Leave this row blank if you did not have to help your partner understand the words.)				
I wrote the turning point sentence carefully and accurately.				

REREAD

Reread "Middle School Loneliness." After you reread, complete the Using Language and Meaningful Interactions activities.

⚙ USING LANGUAGE CA-CCSS: ELD.PII.6.6.Ex

Read each sentence. Choose the correct conjunction to combine the sentences.

1. I was the captain of the basketball team, _____ I was president of the math club.

   ○ and   ○ so   ○ but

2. One summer, my dad accepted a job in a different city, _____ we moved.

   ○ but   ○ so   ○ or

3. I could join the basketball team, _____ I could find something else to do.

   ○ so   ○ or   ○ and

4. I was supposed to make some baskets, _____ I made many.

   ○ or   ○ so   ○ but

5. They treated me badly, _____ we couldn't lose great players.

   ○ but   ○ or   ○ so

Please note that excerpts and passages in the StudySync® library and this workbook are intended as touchstones to generate interest in an author's work. The excerpts and passages do not substitute for the reading of entire texts, and StudySync® strongly recommends that students seek out and purchase the whole literary or informational work in order to experience it as the author intended. Links to online resellers are available in our digital library. In addition, complete works may be ordered through an authorized reseller by filling out and returning to StudySync® the order form enclosed in this workbook.

Reading & Writing Companion 73

MEANINGFUL INTERACTIONS CA-CCSS: ELD.PI.6.10.b.Ex

Use the speaking frames below to summarize "Middle School Loneliness." Only the main events of the story should be included in the summary. Work in small groups to practice sharing and discussing your summary. Then, use the self-assessment rubric to evaluate your participation in the discussion.

- First, the boy . . . because . . .

- The boy felt . . . about the move because . . .

- When the boy got to his new school, he felt . . . because . . .

- Next, the boy decided to . . . because . . .

- Playing on the team was . . . because . . .

- After a while the boy discovered that . . . so he decided to . . .

- In the end, the boy . . .

 SELF-ASSESSMENT RUBRIC CA-CCSS: ELD.PI.6.10.b.Ex

	4 I did this well.	3 I did this pretty well.	2 I did this a little bit.	1 I did not do this.
I summarized the text clearly using complete sentences and main events.				
I listened carefully to others' summaries.				
I spoke respectfully when disagreeing with others.				
I was courteous when persuading others to share my view.				

REREAD

Reread "Middle School Loneliness." After you reread, complete the Using Language and Meaningful Interactions activities.

USING LANGUAGE CA-CCSS: ELD.PII.6.4.Ex

Write adjectives in the blanks to correctly complete the sentence. Use the text if you need help.

1. The boy was captain of a _____ _____ team.

2. My _____ day in the _____ school proved my fears were accurate.

3. The _____ members were_____, _____ friends.

4. Jeremy was _____ captain, and his _____ _____ Nathan was a good player.

5. _____ day I overheard Jeremy and Nathan struggling with an assignment in _____class.

MEANINGFUL INTERACTIONS CA-CCSS: ELD.PI.6.9.Ex, ELD.PI.6.10.b.Ex

Give a summary of "Middle School Loneliness" to the class. Use only the main events from the story, and use complete sentences when presenting your summary. Before presenting, work with a partner to practice sharing and discussing your summary, using the speaking frames and your earlier practice to guide you.

- This story is about . . .

- At his new school . . .

- Then he . . .

- Finally, things get better when . . .

Please note that excerpts and passages in the StudySync® library and this workbook are intended as touchstones to generate interest in an author's work. The excerpts and passages do not substitute for the reading of entire texts, and StudySync® strongly recommends that students seek out and purchase the whole literary or informational work in order to experience it as the author intended. Links to online resellers are available in our digital library. In addition, complete works may be ordered through an authorized reseller by filling out and returning to StudySync® the order form enclosed in this workbook.

Reading & Writing Companion

75

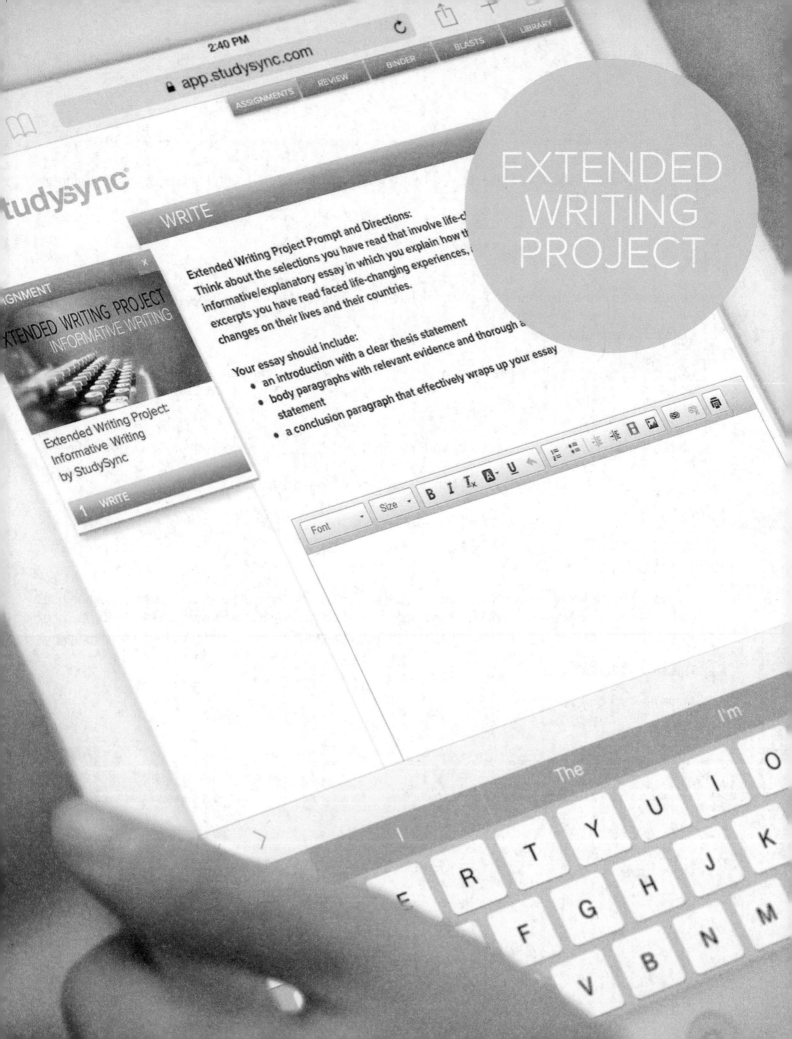

EXTENDED WRITING PROJECT

2:40 PM

app.studysync.com

ASSIGNMENTS REVIEW BINDER BLASTS LIBRARY

studysync®

WRITE

Extended Writing Project Prompt and Directions:

Think about the selections you have read that involve life-ch...

informative/explanatory essay in which you explain how th...

excerpts you have read faced life-changing experiences, ...

changes on their lives and their countries.

Your essay should include:

- an introduction with a clear thesis statement
- body paragraphs with relevant evidence and thorough a...
  statement
- a conclusion paragraph that effectively wraps up your essay

ASSIGNMENT

EXTENDED WRITING PROJECT
INFORMATIVE WRITING

Extended Writing Project:
Informative Writing
by StudySync

1 WRITE

Font   Size   **B** *I* I~x~ A- U

EXTENDED WRITING PROJECT
INFORMATIVE WRITING

INFORMATIVE/
EXPLANATORY
WRITING

WRITING PROMPT

Think about the selections you have read that involve life-changing experiences. Write an informative/explanatory essay in which you explain how three individuals in three of the excerpts you have read faced life-changing experiences, and analyze the impact of these changes on their lives and their countries.

Your essay should include:

- an introduction with a clear thesis statement
- body paragraphs with relevant evidence and thorough analysis to support your thesis statement
- a conclusion paragraph that effectively wraps up your essay

Informative/explanatory writing examines a specific topic and presents ideas and information about it in a logical, organized way. Informative/explanatory writing can explain, define, classify, compare, inform, or describe. Some examples of informative/explanatory writing include: scientific studies, research reports, newspaper or encyclopedia articles, and non-fiction texts such as biographies and histories.

Strong informative/explanatory writing introduces a thesis statement, which is a statement that presents the writer's central (or main) idea about the topic. The writer then develops that thesis statement with relevant supporting details such as facts and examples. The organizational structure of the writing fits the topic, and precise language and clear explanations help the reader understand the information. Transition words not only make the writing flow smoothly but also clarify the relationships among ideas. Though informative/explanatory writing draws a conclusion based on the facts and information, the writing is unbiased, meaning that the writer does not state his/her own opinion.

Please note that excerpts and passages in the StudySync® library and this workbook are intended as touchstones to generate interest in an author's work. The excerpts and passages do not substitute for the reading of entire texts, and StudySync® strongly recommends that students seek out and purchase the whole literary or informational work in order to experience it as the author intended. Links to online resellers are available in our digital library. In addition, complete works may be ordered through an authorized reseller by filling out and returning to StudySync® the order form enclosed in this workbook.

Reading & Writing
Companion

77

NOTES

The features of informative/explanatory writing include:

- a logical organizational structure
- an introduction with a clear thesis statement
- relevant supporting details
- precise language and domain-specific vocabulary
- citations of sources
- a concluding statement

As you continue with this Extended Writing Project, you'll receive more instructions and practice to help you craft each of the elements of informative/explanatory writing in your own essay.

 STUDENT MODEL

Before you get started on your own informative/explanatory essay, begin by reading this essay that one student wrote in response to the writing prompt. As you read this Student Model, highlight and annotate the features of informative/explanatory writing that the student included in the essay.

The Power of Change

Turning points in life are often difficult and challenging times. This idea is explored in the memoir *Warriors Don't Cry* by Melba Pattillo Beals, the autobiography *I Never Had It Made* by Jackie Robinson, and the article "The Father of Chinese Aviation" by Rebecca Maksel. Melba Pattillo Beals, Jackie Robinson, and Feng Ru all faced life-changing experiences and, in doing so, changed their countries.

Melba Pattillo Beals helped improve education for all African American students. She was a student who chose to be one of the first African Americans to integrate Central High in Little Rock, Arkansas. On the morning of September 25,1957, Beals was greeted by "fifty uniformed soldiers" (Beals). They were there to keep her, along with eight other African American students, safe on the first day of school. The threat of violence was very real. Even some adults who supported the students cried openly with fear. Still, Beals was determined to take forward steps for both herself and her people. "Step by step we climbed upward— where none of my people had ever before walked as a student" (Beals). In the face of threats, Beals and the other courageous African American students with her on that day paved the way for new racial attitudes in the United States.

Like Beals, Jackie Robinson also charted new territory for his race. He became the first African American to play major league baseball. In his autobiography, Robinson discussed some of the difficulties he faced. Because he was black, Robinson was not immediately accepted by the team. He had to "live with snubs and rebuffs and rejections" (Robinson). However, the resentment from players on other teams was even worse than from his own team members. Like Beals, he faced threats of violence and "even out-and-out attempts at physical harm" (Robinson). Despite the threats, many African Americans came out to support him. In time, acceptance for Robinson increased, and he took his place as the first of many African American ballplayers. Robinson recognized that this was an important step for African Americans. He was proud, Robinson said, "to prove that a sport can't be called national if blacks are barred from it." Robinson helped change the attitudes of major league baseball. He also helped change the attitudes of his country.

Like Beals and Robinson, Feng Ru's hard work and courage changed his own country—China. Feng Ru was an immigrant to the United States. He was also a self-taught engineer. As a young man, he learned "all he could about machines, working in shipyards, power plants, machine shops" (Maksel). After awhile, he became fascinated with the new field of aviation. In 1906, he started his own "aircraft factory, building airplanes of his own design" (Maksel). However, testing new aircraft was dangerous. During a test flight, Feng lost control of the plane "which plunged into his workshop, setting it ablaze" (Maksel). Although this would not be his last crash, he did not give up his experiments. He returned to China to bring his knowledge of aviation to that country. Feng Ru died in a crash in his homeland, but to this day, he is heralded as the "father of Chinese aviation" (Maksel).

Beals, Robinson, and Feng Ru each faced obstacles and danger. Beals faced an angry mob. Robinson faced threats of violence. Feng Ru faced death itself. However, all three acted with courage, and their determination had an impact on their countries as a whole. Each individual's choices led to a greater good.

Please note that excerpts and passages in the StudySync® library and this workbook are intended as touchstones to generate interest in an author's work. The excerpts and passages do not substitute for the reading of entire texts, and StudySync® strongly recommends that students seek out and purchase the whole literary or informational work in order to experience it as the author intended. Links to online resellers are available in our digital library. In addition, complete works may be ordered through an authorized reseller by filling out and returning to StudySync® the order form enclosed in this workbook.

Reading & Writing Companion

79

THINK QUESTIONS

1. Which sentence in the first two paragraphs most clearly states what the entire essay will be about?

2. In the second paragraph, what evidence does the writer use to support the statement that "Melba Pattillo Beals helped improve education for all African American students"?

3. In the final paragraph of the essay, what conclusions does the writer make about these three individuals and their experiences? Write two or three sentences that sum up in your own words the writer's conclusion.

4. Thinking about the writing prompt, which selections or other resources would you like to use to create your own informative/explanatory essay?

5. Based on what you have read, listened to or researched, how would you answer the question: *What happens when life changes direction?* Explain what you believe are some challenges associated with life changes.

PREWRITE

CA-CCSS: CA.RI.6.1, CA.W.6.2a, CA.W.6.2b, CA.W.6.5, CA.SL.6.1a, CA.SL.6.1b, CA.SL.6.1c, CA.SL.6.1d

WRITING PROMPT

Think about the selections you have read that involve life-changing experiences. Write an informative/explanatory essay in which you explain how three individuals in three of the excerpts you have read faced life-changing experiences, and analyze the impact of these changes on their lives and their countries.

Your essay should include:

- an introduction with a clear thesis statement
- body paragraphs with relevant evidence and thorough analysis to support your thesis statement
- a conclusion paragraph that effectively wraps up your essay

In addition to studying techniques authors use to convey information, you have been reading and learning about stories that feature life-changing experiences. In the Extended Writing Project, you will use informational writing techniques to compose your own informative/explanatory essay.

Since the topic of your informative/explanatory essay will have to do with the impact of life-changing experiences, you'll want to consider how the people you've read about have been impacted by the turning points in their lives. Think back to what you read about Jackie Robinson in *I Never Had It Made*: What important life decision did Robinson face? What were the circumstances of the decision? How easy was the decision to make? What happened as a result of his decision? What did the decision teach him about life? How did his experiences and his reactions to them impact his country?

Please note that excerpts and passages in the StudySync® library and this workbook are intended as touchstones to generate interest in an author's work. The excerpts and passages do not substitute for the reading of entire texts, and StudySync® strongly recommends that students seek out and purchase the whole literary or informational work in order to experience it as the author intended. Links to online resellers are available in our digital library. In addition, complete works may be ordered through an authorized reseller by filling out and returning to StudySync® the order form enclosed in this workbook.

Reading & Writing Companion

81

Make a list of the answers to these questions for Robinson and at least two other individuals you've read about in this unit. As you write down your ideas, look for patterns that begin to emerge. Do the experiences have anything in common? Do you notice ideas that are repeated? Looking for these patterns may help you solidify the ideas you want to discuss in your essay. Use this model to help you get started with your own prewriting:

Text: _I Never Had It Made_, by Jackie Robinson

Life Decision: Robinson decided to fight to be the first African American player in major league baseball.

What Happened: He faced discrimination from both his fellow ballplayers and fans.

In the face of resentment and threats, he proved to be a remarkable baseball player. Eventually, many of the players on his team accepted him, and he drew strength from his relationships with Mr. Rickey and his wife, Rachel.

DEFINE

The **thesis statement** is the most important sentence in an informative/ explanatory essay because it introduces what the writer is going to say about the essay's topic. The thesis statement expresses the writer's central or main idea about that topic, a position the writer will develop in the body of the essay. The thesis statement usually appears in the essay's introductory paragraph and is often the introduction's last sentence. The rest of the paragraphs in the essay all support the thesis statement with facts, evidence, and examples.

IDENTIFICATION AND APPLICATION

A thesis statement:

- makes a clear statement about the writer's central idea
- lets the reader know what to expect in the body of the essay
- responds fully and completely to an essay prompt
- is presented in the introduction paragraph

MODEL

The following is the introduction paragraph from the Student Model, "The Power of Change":

> *Turning points in life are often difficult and challenging times. This idea is explored in the memoir Warriors Don't Cry by Melba Pattillo Beals, the autobiography I Never Had It Made by Jackie Robinson, and the article "The Father of Chinese Aviation" by Rebecca Maksel.* **Melba Pattillo Beals, Jackie Robinson, and Feng Ru all faced life-changing experiences and, in doing so, changed their countries.**

Copyright © BookheadEd Learning, LLC

Notice the bold-faced thesis statement. This student's thesis statement responds to the prompt. It reminds readers of the topic of the essay—the impact of life-changing experiences. It also specifically states the writer's central or main idea about that topic. The writer asserts that Beals, Robinson, and Feng Ru all faced these kinds of amazing experiences, and that both they and their countries were affected by them.

 PRACTICE

Write a thesis statement for your informative/explanatory essay that introduces your central idea in relation to the essay prompt. When you are finished, trade with a partner and offer each other feedback. How clear was the writer's central idea? Is it obvious what this essay will focus on? Does your thesis statement specifically address the prompt? Offer each other suggestions, and remember that they are most helpful when they are constructive.

SKILL:
ORGANIZE
INFORMATIVE
WRITING

 DEFINE

The purpose of writing an informative/explanatory text is to inform readers, so authors need to organize and present their ideas, facts, details, and other information in a logical way. Experienced authors carefully choose an **organizational structure** that best suits their material. They often use an outline or other graphic organizer to determine which organizational structure will help them express their ideas effectively.

For example, scientific reports and studies often use a cause and effect structure. This mirrors the information scientists need to relay—the experiment and the results of the experiment. Historians and memoirists often use a chronological structure, discussing events in the order they occurred. Other organizational structures include: **comparison-contrast, problem-solution, definition, classification,** and **order of importance.**

 IDENTIFICATION AND APPLICATION

- When selecting an organizational structure, writers must consider the purpose of their writing. They often ask themselves questions about the kind of information they are writing about. They might consider:
  - › "What is the central idea I'd like to convey?"
  - › "Would it make sense to relay events in the order they occurred?"
  - › "Is there a specific problem discussed in the texts? What solutions seem likely answers to the problem?"
  - › "Is there a natural cause and effect relationship in my information?"
  - › "Can I compare and contrast different events or individuals' responses to events?"
  - › "Am I teaching readers how to do something?"

- Writers often use word choice to create connections and transitions between ideas and to suggest the organizational structure being used:
  › Sequential order: *first, next, then, finally, last, initially, ultimately*
  › Cause and effect: *because, accordingly, as a result, effect, so*
  › Compare and contrast: *like, unlike, also, both, similarly, although, while, but, however*

- Sometimes, within the overall structure, writers may find it necessary to organize individual paragraphs using other structures - a definition paragraph in a chronological structure, for instance. This should not affect the overall organization.

- Sometimes a writer may include special formatting elements in an informative/explanatory text if these are useful in clarifying organization. These elements may include headings, or phrases in bold that announce the start of a section of text. Headings are usually included only if called for in a prompt or when needed to guide a reader through a long or complex text.

 MODEL

The writer of the Student Model understood from her prewriting that she was mostly comparing and contrasting the life-changing experiences of three different figures in history.

In this excerpt from the introduction of the Student Model, the writer makes the organizational structure clear with her word choice:

> *Like Beals and Robinson, Feng Ru's hard work and courage changed his own country—China.*

The writer uses the word "like" to identify something the three subjects (Beals, Robinson, and Feng Ru) had in common.

The writer of the Student Model, "The Power of Change," knew that she was comparing and contrasting crucial turning points in the lives of three historic figures. She used a three-column chart to organize her ideas during her prewriting process. She color-coded the information so that it was clear what either two or all three of the figures had in common. What was unique to each individual is unmarked.

MELBA PATTILLO BEALS	JACKIE ROBINSON	FENG RU
One of Little Rock 9	Changed their country	Determination
Threat of danger	Played major league baseball	Built planes of his own design
Integrated Central High	Had courage	Changed their country
African American	The first to integrate an institution	Self-taught
Changed their country	Team did not initially support him	Asian
Many people were against it	Determination	Threat of danger
Had courage	African American community supported him	Brought aviation to homeland of China
The first to integrate an institution	African American	Had courage
Determination	Threat of danger	
Death threats	Death threats	
African American community supported her		

 PRACTICE

Using an *Organize Informative/Explanatory Writing* Three-Column Chart like the one you have just studied, fill in the information you've gathered during your prewriting process.

SKILL:
SUPPORTING
DETAILS

 DEFINE

In informative/explanatory writing, writers develop their thesis statement with relevant information called **supporting details.** Relevant information can be any fact, definition, concrete detail, example, or quotation that is important to the reader's understanding of the topic and closely related to the thesis, or central idea. Supporting details can be found in a variety of places, but they must develop the thesis statement in order to be considered relevant and necessary:

- Facts important to understanding the topic
- Research related to the thesis statement
- Quotations from texts or from individuals such as experts or eyewitnesses
- Conclusions of scientific findings and studies
- Definitions from reference material

Writers can choose supporting details from many sources. Encyclopedias, research papers, newspaper articles, graphs, memoirs, biographies, criticism, documentaries, and online references can all provide relevant information for source material. Though information is plentiful and the source material varied, the writer must be careful to evaluate the quality of information to determine what information is most important and most closely related to the thesis statement. If the information doesn't support the topic or if the information doesn't strengthen the writer's point, it is not relevant.

 IDENTIFICATION AND APPLICATION

Step 1:

Review your thesis statement. To identify relevant supporting details, ask this question: What is my central or main idea about this topic? A writer might be making a statement about rainforests, for example:

Copyright © BookheadEd Learning, LLC

We all have a responsibility to save the rainforests.

Step 2:

Ask what a reader needs to know about the topic in order to understand the central idea. In order to understand a statement about *saving* the rainforests, much less the reader's *responsibility* towards them, a reader must first know something about the rainforests. Why do they need saving? In a sentence following, the writer explains this:

They are in *danger* due to our shared use of their resources.

He or she then supplies the reason why:

Rainforests are being harvested for their resources at a rate too fast for them to replenish themselves.

What could that possibly mean to a reader? The writer gives more information:

We use vast amounts of its resources for fuel and clothes.

Step 3:

Look for facts, quotations, research, and the conclusions of others. They will strengthen the thesis statement. It is a building process. Build your information onto the information you gave in the sentence before. Identify supporting details. Carefully evaluate their relevance to your main idea. Ask yourself:

- Is this information necessary to the reader's understanding of the topic?
- Does this information help to prove my point?
- Does this information relate closely to my thesis statement?
- Is there stronger evidence that makes the same point?

 MODEL

In the following excerpt from Jackie Robinson's autobiography *I Never Had It Made*, Robinson develops the idea that Mr. Rickey's motives to let Jackie play in the major leagues were not primarily monetary.

> Mr. Rickey stands out as the man who inspired me the most. He will always have my admiration and respect. Critics had said, "Don't you know that your precious Mr. Rickey didn't bring you up out of the black leagues because he loved you? Are you stupid enough not to understand that the Brooklyn club profited hugely because of what your Mr. Rickey did?"

Yes, I know that. But I also know what a big gamble he took. A bond developed between us that lasted long after I had left the game. In a way I feel I was the son he had lost and he was the father I had lost.

There was more than just making money at stake in Mr. Rickey's decision. I learned that his family was afraid that his health was being undermined by the resulting pressures and that they pleaded with him to abandon the plan. His peers and fellow baseball moguls exerted all kinds of influence to get him to change his mind. Some of the press condemned him as a fool and a demagogue. But he didn't give in.

In paragraph 1, Robinson addresses what the critics said about Mr. Rickey's motives being all about money. He counters with supporting details about Mr. Rickey in paragraphs 2 and 3.

In paragraph 2, Robinson states that he and Mr. Rickey had a bond. This may be true, but Robinson does not provide much concrete evidence here.

Robinson's most compelling evidence of Mr. Rickey's pure motives appears in paragraph 3. He says Mr. Rickey's family worried about his health, Mr. Rickey was pressured by his peers, and he was called a fool by the press. These are three significant and relevant details. They certainly help prove that Mr. Rickey's motives were not strictly monetary.

 PRACTICE

Using sources, write a few supporting details for your informative/explanatory essay that will help develop your thesis statement. List your details on a *Supporting Details* Relevancy Graphic Organizer to determine how strong your supporting details are. Then trade your details with a partner when you are finished. Offer feedback about the details. Engage in a peer review to determine which details are most relevant and strengthen your thesis statement.

EXTENDED WRITING PROJECT
PLAN

PLAN

CA-CCSS: CA.RI.6.1, CA.W.6.2a, CA.W.6.2b, CA.W.6.5, CA.W.6.10, CA.SL.6.1c

WRITING PROMPT

Think about the selections you have read that involve life-changing experiences. Write an informative/explanatory essay in which you explain how three individuals in three of the excerpts you have read faced life-changing experiences, and analyze the impact of these changes on their lives and their countries.

Your essay should include:

- an introduction with a clear thesis statement
- body paragraphs with relevant evidence and thorough analysis to support your thesis statement
- a conclusion paragraph that effectively wraps up your essay

Review the information you listed in your *Organize Informative/Explanatory Writing* Three-Column Chart listing three individuals and the details about the life-changing event or events they experienced. Review the impact of this event on their lives and their country. This organized information, your thesis statement, and your *Supporting Details* Relevancy Graphic Organizer will help you to create a road map to use for writing your essay.

Consider the questions you answered in your prewriting assignment as you develop your main paragraph topics and their supporting details in the road map:

- What important life decision did each person face?
- What were the circumstances of each person's decision?
- How easy was the decision to make?
- What happened as a result of each of these decisions?

- What did these decisions teach the individuals who made them about life?
- How did these experiences and decisions impact the society and country in which these individuals lived?

Use this model to get started with your road map. In each category, write a brief description of the information you plan to include in your informative/ explanatory essay. Write your thesis statement, the topics of each of your paragraphs, and the most relevant supporting details in each paragraph:

Essay Road Map

Thesis statement:

Paragraph 1 Topic:

    Supporting Detail #1:

    Supporting Detail #2:

Paragraph 2 Topic:

    Supporting Detail #1:

    Supporting Detail #2:

Paragraph 3 Topic:

    Supporting Detail #1:

    Supporting Detail #2:

SKILL:
INTRODUCTIONS

 DEFINE

The **introduction** is the opening paragraph or section of a nonfiction text. In an informative/explanatory text, the introduction provides readers with important information by **introducing the topic** and **stating the thesis** that will be developed in the body of the text. A strong introduction also generates interest in the topic by engaging readers in an interesting or attentive way.

 IDENTIFICATION AND APPLICATION

- In informative or explanatory writing, the introduction identifies the topic of the writing by explicitly stating what the text will be about. The writer may also use the introduction to provide some necessary background information about the topic to help the reader understand the information that is to come.

- In addition to the topic, the introduction includes the central, or main, idea that the writer will include in the text. This central idea is the **thesis.** A strong statement of the thesis serves as a guide for the remainder of the work. It lets the reader know what the focus of the essay is. The thesis statement should indicate the point the writer will make and the people or source materials he or she will discuss. Note, however, that a thesis is not always stated explicitly within the text. A writer might instead hint at the thesis through details and ideas in the introduction.

- It is customary to build interest in the topic by beginning the introduction with a **"hook,"** or a way to grab the reader's attention. This awakens the reader's natural curiosity and encourages him or her to read on. Hooks can ask open-ended questions, make connections to the reader or to life, or introduce a surprising fact.

MODEL

Take a look at the introduction of Jackie Robinson's *I Never Had It Made:*

> **I guess if I could choose one of the most important moments in my life, I would go back to 1947, in the Yankee Stadium in New York City.** It was the opening day of the world series and I was for the first time playing in the series as a member of the Brooklyn Dodgers team. **It was a history-making day.** It would be the first time that a black man would be allowed to participate in a world series. **I had become the first black player in the major leagues.**

Jackie Robinson starts readers off with a **hook**. The opening sentence transports the reader back in time, and the reader is left to wonder, "What important thing happened in 1947?" This is an effective hook because the reader will be inclined to read on to discover the answer to this question.

The remainder of the first paragraph in this passage of *I Never Had It Made* goes on to introduce the topic: Robinson was the first black man to play major league baseball. This information appears at the end of the introductory paragraph and is explicitly stated: "I had become the first black player in the major leagues."

The **central idea,** however, is only hinted at in the introduction. The main idea of this passage is that as "the first black player in the major leagues," Jackie Robinson had to overcome many challenges, but by doing so, he changed the course of sports history. However, there is no explicitly stated **thesis** here, because this is an excerpt from Robinson's autobiography, which is longer and more complex than an essay someone might write for school. The **thesis** for the entire book would be much longer than a sentence. Instead, Robinson hints at this idea in the introduction when he states, "It was a history-making day."

PRACTICE

Write an introduction for your informative/explanatory essay that includes a hook, the topic, and the thesis statement. When you are finished, trade with a partner and offer each other feedback. How strong is the language of your partner's thesis statement? How clear is the topic? Were you hooked? Offer each other suggestions, and remember that they are most helpful when they are constructive.

Copyright © BookheadEd Learning, LLC

SKILL: BODY PARAGRAPHS AND TRANSITIONS

DEFINE

Body paragraphs are the section of the essay between the introduction and conclusion paragraphs. This is where you support your thesis statement by developing your main points with evidence from the text and analysis. Typically, each body paragraph will focus on one main point or idea to avoid confusing the reader. The main point of each body paragraph must support the thesis statement.

It's important to structure your body paragraph clearly. One strategy for structuring the body paragraph for an informational essay is the following:

Topic sentence: The topic sentence is the first sentence of your body paragraph and clearly states the main point of the paragraph. It's important that your topic sentence develop the main assertion or statement you made in your thesis statement.

Evidence #1: It's important to support your topic sentence with evidence. Evidence can be relevant facts, definitions, concrete details, quotations, or other information and examples.

Analysis/Explanation #1: After presenting evidence to support your topic sentence, you will need to analyze that evidence and explain how it supports your topic sentence and, in effect, your thesis statement.

Evidence #2: Continue to develop your topic sentence with a second piece of evidence.

Analysis/Explanation #2: Analyze this second piece of evidence and explain how it supports your topic sentence and, in effect, your thesis.

Concluding sentence: After presenting your evidence you need to wrap up your main idea and transition to the next paragraph in your conclusion sentence.

NOTES

Transitions are connecting words and phrases that clarify the relationships among ideas in a text. Transitions work at three different levels: within a sentence, between paragraphs, and to indicate organizational structure.

Authors of informative/explanatory texts use transitions to help readers recognize the overall organizational structure. Transitions also help readers make connections among ideas within and across sentences and paragraphs. Also, by adding transition words or phrases to the beginning or end of a paragraph, authors guide readers smoothly through the text.

In addition, transition words and phrases help authors make connections between words within a sentence. Conjunctions such as *and, or,* and *but* and prepositions such as *with, beyond, inside,* show the relationships between words. Transitions help readers understand how words fit together to make meaning.

IDENTIFICATION AND APPLICATION

- Body paragraphs are the section of the essay between the introduction and conclusion paragraphs. The body paragraphs provide the evidence and analysis/explanation needed to support the thesis statement. Typically, writers develop one main idea per body paragraph.
    › A topic sentence clearly states the main idea of that paragraph.
    › Evidence consists of relevant facts, definitions, concrete details, quotations, or other information and examples.
    › Analysis and explanation are needed to explain how the evidence supports the topic sentence.
    › The conclusion sentence wraps up the main point and transitions to the next body paragraph.

- Transition words are a necessary element of a successful piece of informative/explanatory writing.
    › Transition words help readers understand the text structure of an informative/explanatory text. Here are some transition words that are frequently used in three different text structures:
        › Cause-effect: *because, accordingly, as a result, effect, so, for, since*
        › Compare-contrast: *like, unlike, also, both, similarly, although, while, but, however, whereas, conversely, meanwhile, on the contrary, and yet, still*
        › Chronological order: *first, next, then, finally, last, initially, ultimately*

- Transition words help readers understand the flow of ideas and concepts in a text. Some of the most useful transitions are words that indicate that the ideas in one paragraph are building on or adding to those in another. Examples include: *furthermore, therefore, in addition, moreover, by extension, in order to*, etc.

 ## MODEL

The Student Model uses a body paragraph structure to develop the main ideas presented in the thesis statement and also includes transitions to help the reader understand the relationship among ideas in the text.

Read the body paragraphs from the Student Model, "The Power of Change." Look closely at the structure and note the transition words in bold. Think about the purpose of the information presented. Does it effectively develop the main points made in each topic sentence? How do the transition words help you to understand the similarities and differences between these three individuals and their experiences?

> **Melba Pattillo Beals helped improve education for all African American students.** She was a student who chose to be one of the first African Americans to integrate Central High in Little Rock, Arkansas. On the morning of September 25, 1957, Beals was greeted by "fifty uniformed soldiers" (Beals). They were there to keep her, along with eight other African American students, safe on the first day of school. The threat of violence was very real. Even some adults who supported the students cried openly with fear. Still, Beals was determined to take forward steps for both herself and her people. "Step by step we climbed upward—where none of my people had ever before walked as a student" (Beals). **In the face of threats, Beals and the other courageous African American students with her on that day paved the way for new racial attitudes in the United States.**

> **Like** Beals, Jackie Robinson **also** charted new territory for his race. He became the first African American to play major league baseball. In his autobiography, Robinson discussed some of the difficulties he faced. **Because** he was black, Robinson was not immediately accepted by the team. He had to "live with snubs and rebuffs and rejections" (Robinson). **However,** the resentment from players on other teams was even worse than from his own team members. **Like** Beals, he faced threats of violence and "even out-and-out attempts at physical harm" (Robinson). **Despite** the threats, many

African Americans came out to support him. In time, acceptance for Robinson increased, and Jackie took his place as the first of many African American ballplayers. Robinson recognized that this was an important step for African Americans. He was proud, Robinson said, "to prove that a sport can't be called national if blacks are barred from it." Robinson helped change the attitudes of major league baseball. He **also** helped change the attitudes of his country.

Like Beals and Robinson, Feng Ru's hard work and courage changed his own country—China. Feng Ru was an immigrant to the United States. He was **also** a self-taught engineer. As a young man, he learned "all he could about machines, working in shipyards, power plants, machine shops" (Maksel). **After awhile,** he became fascinated with the new field of aviation. In 1906, he started his own "aircraft factory, building airplanes of his own design" (Maksel). **However,** testing new aircraft was dangerous. **During** a test flight, Feng lost control of the plane "which plunged into his workshop, setting it ablaze" (Maksel). **Although** this would not be his last crash, he did not give up his experiments. He returned to China to bring his knowledge of aviation to that country. Feng Ru died in a crash in his homeland, but to this day, he is heralded as the "father of Chinese aviation" (Maksel).

Body paragraph 1 of the Student Model begins by stating, "Melba Pattillo Beals helped improve education for all African American students." This **topic sentence** clearly establishes the main idea this body paragraph will develop. The writer will attempt to show how Beals improved education.

This topic sentence is immediately followed by **evidence.** The writer uses the example that Beals "chose to be one of the first African Americans to integrate Central High" and includes a direct quote from the excerpt to support the topic sentence.

Directly after the quote "fifty uniformed soldiers" (Beals), the writer **explains** the danger associated with the decision to integrate. The writer then presents a second piece of evidence, emphasizing the determination Beals demonstrated, to further develop the main point established in the topic sentence.

The paragraph concludes by stating that "In the face of threats, Beals and the other courageous African American students with her on that day paved the way for new racial attitudes in the United States." This **conclusion sentence** wraps up the paragraph and makes a clear statement about the impact of Beals's decision.

All three body paragraphs use **transitional words** strategically to show relationships among the ideas in each body paragraph. The first sentence of the second body paragraph states "**Like** Beals, Jackie Robinson **also.**" The transitional words "like" and "also" make it clear that the writer is highlighting the similarities between Beals and Robinson.

The writer also uses transition words such as "however", "because", and "despite" within the body paragraphs themselves to help guide the reader as he or she transitions from one sentence to the next.

 PRACTICE

Write one body paragraph for your literary analysis that compares or contrasts the texts selected for your essay. Make sure your paragraph follows the suggested format, starting with a topic sentence. When you are finished, trade with a partner and offer each other feedback. How effective is the topic sentence at stating the main point of the paragraph? How strong is the textual evidence used to support the topic sentence? What is being compared and contrasted in the paragraph? Do transition words help make the compare-and-contrast relationship clear? Offer each other suggestions, and remember that they are most helpful when they are constructive.

SKILL: CONCLUSIONS

 DEFINE

The **conclusion** is the final paragraph or section of a nonfiction text. In an informative/explanatory text, the conclusion brings the discussion to a close. It follows directly from the introduction and body of the text by referring back to the main ideas presented there. A conclusion should reiterate the thesis statement and summarize the main ideas covered in the body of the text. Depending on the type of text, a conclusion might also include a recommendation or solution, a call to action, or an insightful statement. Many conclusions try to connect with readers by encouraging them to apply what they have learned from the text to their own lives.

 IDENTIFICATION AND APPLICATION

- An effective informative conclusion reinforces the thesis statement.
- An effective informative conclusion briefly mentions or reviews the strongest supporting facts or details. This reminds readers of the most relevant information and evidence in the work.
- The conclusion leaves the reader with a final thought. In informative writing, this final thought may:
  - › Answer a question posed by the introduction
  - › Ask a question on which the reader can reflect
  - › Ask the reader to take action on an issue
  - › Present a last, compelling example
  - › Convey a memorable or inspiring message
  - › Spark curiosity and encourage readers to learn more

MODEL

 NOTES

In the concluding paragraph of the student model "The Power of Change," the writer reinforces the thesis statement, reminds the reader of relevant details, and ends with a final thought.

> **Beals, Robinson, and Feng Ru each faced obstacles and danger.** *Beals faced an angry mob. Robinson faced threats of violence. Feng Ru faced death itself. However,* **all three acted with courage,** *and their determination* **had an impact on their countries as a whole.** *Each individual's* **choices led to a greater good.**

According to the thesis statement, Melba Pattillo Beals, Jackie Robinson, and Feng Ru all faced crucial life-changing experiences, and these changes had an impact on the countries in which they lived. The first line of the conclusion mentions all three historical figures again and reminds the reader of the challenges they faced. Relevant facts in the next few sentences highlight the specific danger each person confronted. Then the writer states that "their determination had an impact on their countries as a whole." This sentence emphasizes the significant changes each person brought about. It explicitly supports the thesis statement of the essay. Finally, the writer broadens the topic to connect with life today. The writer states, "Each individual's life choices led to a greater good." This is an effective final thought. It represents information that the reader can connect with in his or her own life.

 PRACTICE

Write a conclusion for your informative/explanatory essay. When you are finished, trade with a partner and offer each other feedback. How effectively did the writer reinforce the thesis statement in the conclusion? With what final thought did the writer leave the reader? Offer each other suggestions, and remember that they are most helpful when they are constructive.

Please note that excerpts and passages in the StudySync® library and this workbook are intended as touchstones to generate interest in an author's work. The excerpts and passages do not substitute for the reading of entire texts, and StudySync® strongly recommends that students seek out and purchase the whole literary or informational work in order to experience it as the author intended. Links to online resellers are available in our digital library. In addition, complete works may be ordered through an authorized reseller by filling out and returning to StudySync® the order form enclosed in this workbook.

Reading & Writing Companion

101

NOTES

DRAFT

CA-CCSS: CA.RI.6.1, CA.RI.6.2, CA.W.6.2a, CA.W.6.2b, CA.W.6.2c, CA.W.6.2d, CA.W.6.2f, CA.W.6.5, CA.W.6.10, CA.SL.6.1a, CA.L.6.1c, CA.L.6.6

WRITING PROMPT

Think about the selections you have read that involve life-changing experiences. Write an informative/explanatory essay in which you explain how three individuals in three of the excerpts you have read faced life-changing experiences, and analyze the impact of these changes on their lives and their countries.

Your essay should include:

- an introduction with a clear thesis statement
- body paragraphs with relevant evidence and thorough analysis to support your thesis statement
- a conclusion paragraph that effectively wraps up your essay

You've already made progress toward writing your own informative/ explanatory text. You've thought about your purpose, audience, and topic. You've carefully examined the unit's texts and selected your three individuals. Based on your analysis of textual evidence, you've identified what you want to say about life-changing experiences. You've decided how to organize information, and gathered supporting details. Now it's time to write a draft of your essay.

Use your essay road map and your other prewriting materials to help you as you write. Remember that informative/explanatory writing begins with an introduction and presents a thesis statement. Body paragraphs develop the thesis statement with supporting ideas, details, quotations, and other relevant information and explanations drawn from or based on the texts. Transitions help the reader understand the relationships among ideas and to follow the flow of information. A concluding paragraph restates or reinforces your thesis statement. An effective conclusion can also do more—it can leave a lasting impression on your readers.

Copyright © BookheadEd Learning, LLC

NOTES

Finally, remember that correct use of language is necessary if your readers are going to understand your descriptions and ideas. Your language should be precise, rather than too vague or general, to help your readers follow information and learn about your topic. In some cases, you may want to use specialized vocabulary or domain-specific words, if appropriate, to fit your topic. It is always important to check that you use words that are grammatically correct. One important thing to consider is whether you are using pronouns correctly: if your pronouns do not agree in number or person, or if they shift around throughout the essay, readers may be confused.

When drafting, ask yourself these questions:

- How can I improve my hook to make it more appealing?
- What can I do to clarify my thesis statement?
- What textual evidence—including relevant facts, strong details, and interesting quotations —supports the thesis statement?
- Have I chosen an organizational structure that makes information clear, and that helps readers understand my topic?
- How have I used transitions to clarify the relationships among my ideas?
- Would more precise language or different details about these extraordinary individuals make the text more exciting and vivid? How well have I communicated what these individuals experienced and achieved?
- What final thought do I want to leave with my readers?

Before you submit your draft, read it over carefully. You want to be sure that you've responded to all aspects of the prompt.

REVISE

CA-CCSS: CA.RI.6.1, CA.W.6.2a, CA.W.6.2b, CA.W.6.2c, CA.W.6.2d, CA.W.6.2e, CA.W.6.2f, CA.W.6.4, CA.W.6.5, CA.W.6.10, CA.SL.6.1c, CA.L.6.1b, CA.L.6.1c, CA.L.6.3b

WRITING PROMPT

Think about the selections you have read that involve life-changing experiences. Write an informative/explanatory essay in which you explain how three individuals in three of the excerpts you have read faced life-changing experiences, and analyze the impact of these changes on their lives and their countries.

Your essay should include:
- an introduction with a clear thesis statement
- body paragraphs with relevant evidence and thorough analysis to support your thesis statement
- a conclusion paragraph that effectively wraps up your essay

You have written a draft of your informative/explanatory text. You have also received input from your peers about how to improve it. Now you are going to revise your draft.

Here are some recommendations to help you revise.

- Review the suggestions made by your peers.
- Focus on maintaining a formal style. A formal style suits your purpose—giving information about a serious topic. It also fits your audience—students, teachers, and other readers interested in learning more about your topic.
  › As you revise, eliminate any slang.
  › Remove any first-person pronouns such as "I," "me," or "mine" or instances of addressing readers as "you." These are more suitable to a writing style that is informal, personal, and conversational.

NOTES

> Check that you have used all pronouns correctly, including reflexive and intensive pronouns. Remember that the same kinds of pronouns (ending in -*self* or -*selves*) can be either reflexive or intensive.

> If you include your personal opinions, remove them. Your essay should be clear, direct, and unbiased.

- After you have revised elements of style, think about whether there is anything else you can do to improve your essay's information or organization.

    > Do you need to add any new textual evidence to fully support your thesis statement or engage the interest of readers?

    > Did one of your three individuals say something special that you forgot to quote? Quotations can add life to your essay.

    > Can you substitute a more precise word for a word that is general or dull?

    > Consider your organization. Would your essay flow better if you strengthened the transitions between paragraphs?

    > How effective is your conclusion? Do you want to strengthen it by leaving your readers with a final message?

NOTES

SOURCES AND CITATIONS
sync•skills
Writing

SKILL: SOURCES AND CITATIONS

 ## DEFINE

Sources are the documents and information that an author uses to research his or her writing. Some sources are **primary sources.** A primary source is a first-hand account of thoughts or events by the individual who experienced them. Other sources are **secondary sources.** A secondary source analyzes and interprets primary sources. **Citations** are notes that give information about the sources an author used in his or her writing. Citations are required whenever authors quote others' words or refer to others' ideas in their writing. Citations let readers know who originally came up with those words and ideas.

 ## IDENTIFICATION AND APPLICATION

- Sources can be primary or secondary in nature. Primary sources are first-hand accounts, artifacts, or other original materials. Examples of primary sources include:

  › Letters or other correspondence
  › Photographs
  › Official documents
  › Diaries or journals
  › Autobiographies or memoirs
  › Eyewitness accounts and interviews
  › Audio recordings and radio broadcasts
  › Works of art
  › Artifacts

- Secondary sources are usually text. Secondary sources are the written interpretation and analysis of primary source materials. Some examples of secondary sources include:

  › Encyclopedia articles
  › Textbooks

> › Commentary or criticisms
> › Histories
> › Documentary films
> › News analyses

- Whether sources are primary or secondary, they must be credible and accurate. Writers of informative/explanatory texts look for sources from experts in the topic they are writing about.

  > › When researching online, they look for URLs that contain ".gov" (government agencies), ".edu" (colleges and universities), and ".org" (museums and other non-profit organizations).
  > › Writers also use respected print and online news and information sources.

- When a writer uses sources, he or she usually tells their titles and authors in the introduction to the writing. Notice that the writer of the Student Model names the authors and titles of the selections included in his or her essay in the introduction to "The Power of Change." However, when many sources have been used, or in a formal research report, writers usually also include a Works Cited list at the end of their writing. A Works Cited list includes all the information available about the sources the writer used. You will learn more about preparing a Works Cited list in a later unit.

- Anytime a writer uses words from another source exactly as they are written, the words must appear in quotation marks. Quotation marks show that the words are not the author's own words but are borrowed from another source. In the Student Model, the writer uses quotation marks around words taken directly from the source *Warriors Don't Cry*:

  "Step by step we climbed upward—where none of my people had ever before walked as a student" (Beals).

- A writer includes a citation to give credit to any source, whether primary or secondary, that is quoted exactly. There are several different ways to cite a source. In the Student Model, the writer tells readers exactly what selections are being included in the essay in the introduction. The title and author of each source is

  > › One way is to put the author's last name in parenthesis at the end of the sentence in which the quote appears. This is what the writer of the Student Model does after the quotation above.
  > › Another way to give credit is to cite the author's name in the context of the sentence. For example, in the student model essay, the writer indicates that Robinson himself says these quoted words from *I Never had it Made*.

Please note that excerpts and passages in the StudySync® library and this workbook are intended as touchstones to generate interest in an author's work. The excerpts and passages do not substitute for the reading of entire texts, and StudySync® strongly recommends that students seek out and purchase the whole literary or informational work in order to experience it as the author intended. Links to online resellers are available in our digital library. In addition, complete works may be ordered through an authorized reseller by filling out and returning to StudySync® the order form enclosed in this workbook.

Reading & Writing Companion   **107**

NOTES

He was proud, Robinson said, **"to prove that a sport can't be called national if blacks are barred from it."**

- Citations are also necessary when a writer borrows ideas from another source, even if the writer paraphrases, or puts those ideas in his or her own words. Citations credit the source, but they also help readers discover where they can learn more.
- When writers use and cite sources in research reports, they usually include a Works Cited list at the very end of their writing. A Works Cited list gives complete information about every work.

 MODEL

In this excerpt from the student model essay, the writer uses quotations from secondary source material and includes parenthetical citations.

> Like Beals and Robinson, Feng Ru's hard work and courage changed his own country—China. Feng Ru was an immigrant to the United States. He was also a self-taught engineer. As a young man, he learned **"all he could about machines, working in shipyards, power plants, machine shops" (Maksel).** After awhile, he became fascinated with the new field of aviation. In 1906, he started his own **"aircraft factory, building airplanes of his own design" (Maksel).** However, testing new aircraft was dangerous. During a test flight, Feng lost control of the plane **"which plunged into his workshop, setting it ablaze" (Maksel).** Although this would not be his last crash, he did not give up his experiments. He returned to China to bring his knowledge of aviation to that country. Feng Ru died in a crash in his homeland, but to this day, he is heralded as the **"father of Chinese aviation" (Maksel).**

Notice that each sentence begins with the writer's own words. When the writer uses portions of text from the source material, those specific portions of text appear in quotations. The student has cited material with the author's last name in parenthesis after each quotation.

The quotations in this paragraph all come from an article written by Rebecca Maksel. Because the article is written by Maksel about Feng Ru, a historical figure, and not by Feng Ru himself, this is a secondary source. All references to the secondary source are cited to give credit to the author.

PRACTICE

Write citations for quoted information in your informative/explanatory essay. When you are finished, trade with a partner and offer each other feedback. How successful was the writer in citing sources for the essay? How well did the writer incorporate sources? Did he or she always include them in parentheses at the end of a sentence, or were they sometimes included in the context of the sentence? Did the writer paraphrase some ideas, putting them in his or her own words? If so, did the writer remember to credit the original source of the paraphrased idea? Offer each other suggestions, and remember that they are most helpful when they are constructive.

NOTES

EDIT,
PROOFREAD,
AND PUBLISH

CA-CCSS: CA.W.6.2a, CA.W.6.2b, CA.W.6.2c, CA.W.6.2d, CA.W.6.2e, CA.W.6.2f, CA.W.6.4, CA.W.6.5, CA.W.6.6, CA.W.6.8, CA.W.6.10, CA.SL.6.1a, CA.SL.6.1b, CA.SL.6.1c, CA.SL.6.1d, CA.SL.6.6, CA.L.6.1b, CA.L.6.1c, CA.L.6.2b, CA.L.6.3b

WRITING PROMPT

Think about the selections you have read that involve life-changing experiences. Write an informative/explanatory essay in which you explain how three individuals in three of the excerpts you have read faced life-changing experiences, and analyze the impact of these changes on their lives and their countries.

Your essay should include:

- an introduction with a clear thesis statement
- body paragraphs with relevant evidence and thorough analysis to support your thesis statement
- a conclusion paragraph that effectively wraps up your essay

You have revised your informative/explanatory essay and received input from your peers on that revision. Now it's time to edit and proofread your essay to produce a final version. As you reread your work, think about whether there's anything more you can do to improve it. Keep these questions in mind as you edit your writing, making additional changes as needed:

- Have I included my peers' valuable suggestions?
- Is the style and tone of my writing appropriate for my audience throughout my essay?
- Have I informed my readers about the life-changing experiences of three individuals and explained the impact of those experiences?
- Have I introduced my thesis statement clearly, developed it with strong textual evidence, and reinforced it in my conclusion?
- Does my organizational structure make the information flow smoothly? Do transitions clarify the relationships among my ideas?

NOTES

- Will any of my ideas, facts, or examples be improved if I substitute a more precise word for one that is vague or general?

- Have I accurately cited my sources?

When you are satisfied with the content, style, and organization of your work, proofread your writing carefully for errors. For example, have you used correct punctuation for quotations and citations? Make sure that pronouns agree with their antecedents, and that you have used reflexive and intensive pronouns correctly. Also check that you have eliminated any sentence fragments. Be sure to correct any misspelled words.

Once you have made all your corrections, you are ready to submit and publish your work. You can distribute your writing to family and friends, hang it on a bulletin board, or post it on a blog. If you publish online, create links to your sources and citations. That way, readers can follow-up on what they've learned from your informative/explanatory essay and read more on their own.

Text Fulfillment
Through StudySync

If you are interested in specific titles, please fill out the form below and we will check availability through our partners.

ORDER DETAILS

Date:

TITLE	AUTHOR	Paperback/ Hardcover	Specific Edition *If Applicable*	Quantity

SHIPPING INFORMATION

Contact:

Title:

School/District:

Address Line 1:

Address Line 2:

Zip or Postal Code:

Phone:

Mobile:

Email:

BILLING INFORMATION   ☐ SAME AS SHIPPING

Contact:

Title:

School/District:

Address Line 1:

Address Line 2:

Zip or Postal Code:

Phone:

Mobile:

Email:

PAYMENT INFORMATION

☐ CREDIT CARD   Name on Card:

Card Number: Expiration Date: Security Code:

☐ PO   Purchase Order Number:

StudySync Text Fulfillment, BookheadEd Learning, LLC
610 Daniel Young Drive | Sonoma, CA 95476